Ride It Out

Dr. Corrine Ferereo!
Thank you for the
support! Keep allowing
God to use you in mighty
ways!

RIDE IT OUT

Berry Best Books
Publishing Co.

Book design by Shanté D. Berry Editing: Cherie Banks, V.Girmonde October 2017, First Edition
ISBN 978-0-692-97153-6
An Imprint of Berry Best Books Publishing
www.berrybestpublishing.co
Ordering Information:
Available through Amazon, Barnes and Noble, and Kindle.
Special discounts are available on quantity purchases by corporations, associations, educators, and others. For details, contact the publisher at the above listed address.

Ride It Out

Transforming Storms Into Greatness

Shanté D. Berry

Contents

Foreward

One of my favorite music influencers is three-time Grammy Award-winning singer-songwriter, Jill Scott. Before Jill became known for hitting the Billboard charts, she began her performing career as a spoken word artist. Jill performed at live poetry readings to showcase her creative work. Her soulful lyrics and alluring stage presence led to Jill's discovery.

When I first discovered Shanté Berry, she was a rising spoken word artist. Like Jill Scott, she had a unique way with words. Shanté had the expressive ability to take you into a rhythmic depth of emotion through her rhymes. Her lyricism was raw, riveting, and real. She 'spit' the truth on racism, discrimination, miseducation, poverty, injustice, self-love, and survival. It was evident that Shanté had a calling to be a catalyst for change. If you ask her, Shanté would tell you that change chased her, but I believe she chased it.

At an early age, Shanté survived many of life's storms growing up. As she matured, Shanté faced some of the biggest storms in U.S. history, Hurricane Katrina and Hurricane Harvey. Even though she lost nearly everything, she never surrendered her spirit. Instead, Shanté did what she does best, Ride It Out! She imparts her life lessons in this personal narrative on weathering the storms for greatness.

It's her own story of tragedy, transformation, and triumph. When I traveled with Shanté into the storms of her life between the pages of this memoir, I could not help but think of Jill Scott's 2nd album, Beautifully Human: Words and Sounds Vol. 2. The title of this album describes Shanté's journey from a quirky little girl to a strong, confident woman. Her life reflections are bold and daring as she risks her vulnerabilities and exposes her pain in search of natural beauty, authentic identity, and self-love.

Jill Scott once said, "I think, as an artist, you have to have experienced some deep turmoil, some kind of pain, because that's what connects you with the world." This is also true for Shanté. She has a powerfully unique way of connecting her pain with the world, but she doesn't sit in pain. Instead, Shanté pushes the pain into purpose. Her survival is a testament to the words and sounds of poetic therapy, and God is her saving grace in the spoken word.

I first heard Shanté perform when she stepped on the stage for open mic night at the hottest spot for poetry, jazz, and neo-soul in Phoenix, AZ. It was voted #1 for Best Spoken Word and won several Reader's Choice Awards in multiple categories for consecutive years in a row by Arizona's New Times. It was also voted #1 for Best VIP List & Entertainment by 944 Magazine and is ranked #1 for Best Performing Arts in Culture & Diversity by Arizona Nightlife.

This hot spot happened to be my side hustle. I created the platform, owned the stage, and was one of the Top 5 Influencers in the Valley. My day gig was law, but my passion was poetry. However, my life was people. Instantly,

Shanté had become a part of my life. At the time, she was learning to find her wings, so I covered her in wisdom, knowledge, understanding, and love. She was beautiful to watch and as she grew so did her wings.

I had worked with the best musicians and spoken word artists across the country and around the world. My stage was a sanctuary for HBO Def Poets, international award-winning spoken word artists, nationally acclaimed poet laureates, and local poetry slam winners. These are some of the most impressive minds and meaningful voices who influenced Shanté's creative writing and poetry performance. She was surrounded by greatness. Years later, when Shanté was crowned Miss Black Arizona USA in 2011, I learned that this foundational training was instrumental in her preparation. It also positioned her to achieve other notable professional accomplishments.

I knew that Shanté would be successful in whatever she pursued in life. I knew it the moment she 'dropped the mic' on my stage. Her spoken word poetry raised social consciousness, provoked deep thought, challenged systematic action, and inspired higher hope. Her valuable contributions in this book are no different. She remains steadfast in her determination to create positive change with her words and sounds. Shanté's success is evident because of her refusal to let the storms stop her progress. I can't believe it's been over a decade since I discovered her greatness. Shanté has survived every storm to succeed. Today, she shares her success to help others become successful. That's what makes life golden. I'm sure Jill Scott would agree. Find purpose in the storms. Be encouraged to Ride It Out. Live life like it's golden.

    Cherie Banks, MA, JD

    Business Investor & Enterprise Entrepreneur

    CEO Influencer™

    Dallas, TX

Rising Tides

"We all face storms in life. Some are more difficult than others, but we all go through trials and tribulations, that is why we have the gift of faith."
– Joyce Meyer

The category five storm had made landfall. I could hear the rumbling roof of my dormitory building rattle as if it was about to come off at any given second. Chills ran through my body. I nestled on the hallway floor with my colleagues listening to the wind howl.

Some cried, shouted, and screamed while others fell silent to the mystery of the night. It sounded like a train was coming straight toward us with no brakes. The first thing to go was the power, then the water, and lastly the food. Somehow in the midst of all that, I fell asleep in a fetal position on a crowded floor. When I awoke a few hours later, I walked courageously to a nearby window to witness the devastation. I knew that this is what my mother meant by riding it out.

I tried to escape, but with only a 24-hour emergency evacuation warning I didn't move fast enough.

I had no idea that over the next five days, I would be surrounded in an abyss of black sludge water, army tanks, assault rifles, bloated bodies, and political and economic mayhem better known as Hurricane Katrina. Wait, let's flashback, wayyyy back. How did I get here?

July would NEVER be the same. In the summer of the mid-1980s, a baby girl with chunky cheeks, bright eyes, and a head full of curly hair had been born. Los Angeles gave birth to me, Saint Louis raised me, New Orleans educated me, Phoenix tamed me, and Houston paid me. I was born to fly. I learned to adapt and survive in every city I've ever lived in. It's been amazing and an exciting journey thus far. I have sincere gratitude to God for allowing me to live fully. If you're blessed with one more day on this earth, it's a blessing indeed. Make the most of it and live your life out loud.

My parents made education a top priority. As the only girl in my family, I felt their expectations were set even higher for me than my brothers. When I was accepted into my top college choice in New Orleans, Louisiana nobody in the world had joy like this inner-city girl from the north side of Saint Louis, MO. Triumphant chants and screams resounded from the streets of San Francisco Avenue when I received my acceptance letter. I was ready to see and change the world. I matriculated through three wonderful years in college succeeding to my senior year. It was time to shine!

"Attention all students, classes will be canceled for the next full week." These words jumped off the page as I read the posting on the dormitory elevator door. What now? I thought. The news of Hurricane Katrina was on every television I walked past. When I entered my dorm room, I could see my roommate sitting on her bed watching too.

Just a week ago, it was summer. August passed by swiftly as I prepared for my last year of college. It felt like just yesterday, I was a freshman. For the first time, I had cut my hair. It was perfect for the new school year ahead.

My father and I traveled from the Midwest by car on a twelve-hour expedition to New Orleans. He always drove me to school, but this year was scheduled to be the last. When we arrived at my school for my final year, my dad took me shopping for dorm room necessities. The drop-off was smooth and simple. We said our goodbyes then he rode off into the sunset.

There I stood, a 5'5 young woman with brown eyes and a short curly copper afro waving bye to my father. The start of the semester was an exciting time and I was thrilled to be back amongst my colleagues. It never crossed my mind that the possibility of never seeing him again could soon become a reality or that I would return home to Saint Louis with nothing, but the clothes on my back. The beginning of my senior year became the eve of a horrible natural and political disaster.

Whenever New Orleans had hurricane warnings, I knew the protocol that would follow. When massive storms were in-route, it afforded me opportunities to take spontaneous road trips with friends. I would often visit neighboring states; Alabama, Georgia or Texas. Usually, it was Alabama because my brother attended college in Huntsville. It was the perfect place to go since I could check him out on campus and enjoy the sights of another city. I love New Orleans, but the unpredictability of the weather was serious. I never knew what to expect, and I had little to no experience with hurricanes.

In previous years, there were hurricane warnings bringing heavy rain and a little extra wind. These conditions didn't scare me so I figured Hurricane Katrina would be no different. I didn't play into the hype until I received a call from my parents who lived out-of-state. They knew about the coming of Hurricane Katrina and wanted to know my plans for evacuating. National news, I thought. Hmmm.

As I sat on my dorm room bed, I asked myself, is this worth the energy? I didn't want to waste money by taking another trip out of town for another routine hurricane warning. I've done this in the previous years, and nothing serious ever happened. I was conflicted, but I needed to make a decision fast.

The mayor, Ray Nagin, addressed the city in a very calm manner. I remained silent and weighed my options. I peeked out of my dorm room and saw my colleagues scattered around campus. Suddenly, they were loading themselves into cars as if they have won a surprise vacation. I could hear bags being packed from every direction as car doors slammed and vehicles sped away.

Home for many of my colleagues was only a few hours away or at best the next state over. I envied them because my situation didn't afford me that convenience. I was different, especially since I did not have my car this semester. My mind filled about the possibilities for evacuating, and somehow I fell asleep. A few hours later, I heard a loud "boom" at the door! I panicked and jumped up to see that it was.

My friend, Alana busted in the door, "Shanté, have you been looking at the news?"

"Yea earlier, but I had just woke up. What's going on?"

"Shanté, there is a mandatory evacuation for New Orleans. The mayor announced it!"

My phone lunged off the edge of my desk and hit the floor. It was vibrating and ringing loudly. I picked it up to hear my mother on the line asking, "So what are you going to do?"

I responded, "I'm not sure, but I need to get out of here!"

Within the next 30 minutes, I contacted every mode of transportation in New Orleans from a plane, bus, and train. Everything had already shut down completely. My last hope was to leave by car.

Alana offered to drive me to her hometown, Houston, Texas. However, there was one problem; the highways were backed up to the Superdome. Soon the bridges leaving out of the city were closing at midnight. I glanced out of the window and saw a sea of cars on the highway, idling in frustration, going nowhere. The scene began to get overwhelming. Together, we considered to stay and see what plans the college had for us.

Suddenly, there was something different from the prior evacuation protocols. I received less than a 24-hour notice to get out of town. This left me with no other option, but to stay on campus and follow the faculty's direction. The next day came and went with growing curiosity and fear. In the midst of chaos, my mother managed to get a hold of a faculty member to discuss a rescue plan.

The faculty member informed my mother of the plans for students staying on campus and remaining safe. My mother swelled with frustration as her first choice wasn't for me to stay in New Orleans. She called me back quickly to say, "It looks as if you are going to have to ride it out Shanté." Her only daughter was stranded in a city with a massive hurricane coming straight toward her. My mom knew too well what riding it out meant. This was a catch phrase I was taught over my lifetime.

As the storm moved in closer the day finally came to an end. Early the next morning, New Orleans was bracing for the storm to hit. The school announced that students would be in one dormitory, needed to pack one bag, and meet at the entrance in one hour.

How could I be this unlucky, unfortunate, and lost in time where I could not get out of town? What about the citizens of New Orleans who didn't have the means to get out? Were people unwilling to uproot themselves since past storms didn't pose such serious threats? Was it the lack of money that kept them in the city or the short time frame to evacuate that kept them home? I thought about New Orleans and the thousands of people like me who had no other option, but to stay.

The remaining students and faculty on campus gathered in the lobby. Just before sunset, I felt a sweaty hand reaching for mine. One of my colleagues wanted me to join the prayer circle forming in the middle of the room. We bowed our heads in solidarity, prayed for our safety, sanity, the safety of our school, the city of New Orleans, and people that did not have adequate shelter. I could feel the thickness of tension spreading in the room as the storm was only a few hundred miles away.

The next night we migrated to the fifth floor and had a brief meeting about what was supposed to happen. We were restricted from the dorm rooms because of the danger of the glass windows shattering. I turned my bed comforter into a nest on the floor hoping to rest.

On the morning of August 29, 2005, at approximately 4:15AM, Hurricane Katrina made landfall. The wind blew with a vengeance at 175 miles per hour claiming a category five storm. One of the worst in U.S. history. The extreme howl of the wind resounded around the walls and doors of the dormitory. The six-story building felt more and more like an island. We huddled together on the hallway floor, some in silence, some telling stories, and others praying. Everyone tried to keep each other's spirits up. I then fell into a light sleep as the storm ravaged the city. I could hear the whirling winds fading in and out while I slept.

Once I woke up, I walked to the window down the hall. The aggressive winds looked like ocean waves elevated into the air. I saw the wind blowing as it ripped through the city and tossed trees and branches around like loose leaves. I was shocked to personally witness the eye of the storm right in front of me. It was both breathtaking and frightening. A few other classmates stood next to me. I pressed my warm hand against the window, and it became cold as ice. The thick glass window was the only barrier between me and one of the most horrific and deadliest American storms.

Torrential rains poured the following day. Later on, a variety of dry food items and water became accessible, but I couldn't eat anything. I didn't have an appetite. Stress left no room for hunger. Instead, there was a different type of hunger rising inside of me.

As this day came to an end, the conditions seemed to neutralize. The hurricane officially passed over, and it was finally peaceful. I thanked God for another day to live, and I was eager to go home. Little did I know that home was another week or so away. I was barricaded in this dormitory building with no means of escape. Even though I was able to sleep for a little while, I was living a nightmare. I had an intense concern as the faculty grew silent with the day-to-day direction of my life.

"It's over already. Let's go home!" "What are they waiting for?"

This question swirled through the hallways of the building. I knew that something was wrong. Why are we still here? Nearly two hundred students circled around the dormitory with increasing tension. What was going on? The storm is over!!! As the sun started to shine outside, I was left in utter darkness.

What was taking the nation so long to provide emergency relief and re-open the city again? Was I being punished for staying and even more for surviving? By Wednesday, another day unfolded the saddening reality that I wasn't going home. The city remained in quiet despair. I continued to wait for direction, disaster relief, and for New Orleans to be back up and running again.

The next morning, the day stretched more time, just enough for the city's atmosphere to change with unprecedented conflict. What was new hope after the storm with tranquility floating in the blue sky above, merely masked the tragedy that awaited me. Suddenly, I woke up to a severe shift in the water level. The parking lot outside had transformed into a black ocean, dark and murky. Alana's car was completely submerged in water. As the hours went by, I couldn't see the stop sign at the corner any longer. I panicked as the water kept rising higher. The levees broke down, but no one informed us.

"What are the plans?" I asked my colleagues. Who is coming for us? Why are we still here?" However, there were no answers. The look on their faces inferred that they had the same questions in their head. I felt like I was all on my own.

For the next two days, I was in disbelief that New Orleans remained under water and nobody came to help. I believed that no one cared and none of our lives mattered. The hardest thing I was forced to tolerate was the unsanitary conditions. Without running water or power, no one could take showers and using the bathroom was a daunting task. The heavy fumes of toxic human waste lingered in my upper nostrils. The feces marinating in nearby toilets couldn't flush. I had no choice but to breathe in the dreadful stench.

The air quality smelled like a porter potty that had been microwaved from the sun. The putrid smell was grotesque, often causing me to want to vomit. This will forever be an unforgettable trauma in my life.

Other students grew beyond impatient with waiting. They started making plans to escape while I sat and pondered different outcomes. Eventually, we rallied together and agreed to go to the Superdome, about three miles away. "Let's load up the relief food, water, and blankets." Bad idea. Three miles away, thousands of people were fighting for the same relief. However, the shelter conditions at the Superdome were severely compromised.

It was now days after Hurricane Katrina. By this time, I was hopeless, but my faith wouldn't let me remain that way. I thought about my education, family, goals, and all the things important to me. I said to myself, when I make it out of this, I will be stronger and capable of anything!

It had been nearly a week since I spoke to my parents. The last thing I remember was sending them a text right before my phone lost a signal and power. #TheWaterIsRisingWeNeedHelp!!!

During the vast and deadly whitespace between us, my mother somehow worked behind the scenes to get the Louisiana governor's secretary personally involved in my rescue while my dad was putting a deposit on a boat. They possessed unconditional love for me and unrelenting faith in God. I knew that my parents were coming for me through hell or high water! That evening, my mother's call miraculously got through the airwaves once my phone regained power. She said, "Shanté, the Secretary of the State will call you in five minutes to pick up."

I asked no questions. "Okay," I replied.

A sharp and faint voice came through on my phone minutes later. "Hello, Shanté are you ok?"

"No, we need help," as my voice shook. "It's about two hundred of us, and we need help!"

I don't know how I was talking on the phone at this point. No one else had a signal or power. Just by hearing that lady's voice comforted me with relief. I felt one step closer to going home. That night I collapsed hard on my knees. I asked God to protect us and help us find a way back home. I prayed for a sense of normalcy for my beloved city, New Orleans.

The next morning, carried distant echoes of an explosion that awakened me. There was a loud, BOOM! My heart was beating rapidly and lost its rhythm. What I thought was a mirage turned into a miracle. I noticed a medium-sized boat from my window. I jumped up! At last, I'm going to go home! I had no idea if they were coming for me, but I knew that they were going to hear me! I pried open the window with the help of my classmates, and we all started yelling, "HELLLLLP! HELLLLLLP! PLEASE HELLLLLLPPP US!!!!"

Within seconds, we bolted downstairs with our belongings. They were there for us. The faculty instructed to bring one personal item then line up by the door. It was surreal. Was I really about to go home? Just like that? It was the best blessing of all my days, but what a long day it would be.

This was it. I was finally on my journey home. Not one, but two medium-sized boats rowed up as close to the dormitory building as possible. The boats could only make it partially up the ramp so we had to meet them halfway. The olive greenish dark murky water was the only thing that separated me from the boats. I rolled up my pants leg and inched toward one of the boats. I couldn't see the bottom of the ground and all I could think about was the bloated bodies I saw bobbing and floating from afar. What if I tripped over someone?

Cringing, I put the thought out of my mind and continued to tread through the graveyard of water underneath my shoulders. Slowly, I made my way to the boat, which made multiple trips to the highway and back. It loaded and transported nearly two hundred students to a safe location. We stood as one on the overpass at highway 10 to do one thing, WAIT!

I didn't know what was next to come. Again, no specific directions were given. I stood for hours then walked to stretch my legs and eventually sat down due to exhaustion. Nine in the morning transitioned into five o'clock in the afternoon, and I grew very hungry.

Out of nowhere, I heard a loud rapid turbo helicopter overhead. Meal ready-to-eat packages in tan colored bags were dropped down. These were the same dry food packages that the military used at war. I was puzzled. What should I do with it? When I opened it, I found contents of beef stew, rice, peas, crackers, Gatorade powdered juice, M&M's, salt and pepper, and lastly, hot sauce. There was also a flameless rotation heater so I could add water to a bag that would cook the food without heat. I was amazed. Very interesting diet indeed. I had enjoyed eating what I could.

Later, I saw tanks trekking slowly through the murky flood water and onto dry land. One of the tanks transported me to where three huge charter buses were awaiting my arrival with almost 200 students by my side. We marched off the tank like an army ready to go to war. When we gathered around the charter buses, the doors flew open, and there was Reverend Jesse Jackson! I was shocked to see him making his way down the stairs of the charter bus. He stood over six feet tall with broad shoulders and a stern demeanor.

Every student cheered in excitement! Here was a civil rights leader right in front of us who cared for our safety and wanted to be with us in our time of despair. He had a vigorous look of concern and seriousness. At that moment, Reverend Jackson showed me that my life mattered. It was extremely surreal. For the first time in that entire week, I felt a magnitude of emotions stirring inside of me from the heavy rainfall, thrusting winds, and damage of Hurricane Katrina. I could not help but stare at Reverend Jackson in awe.

Then he said, "Repeat after me, "I AM SOMEBODY!" We all shouted, "I AM SOMEBODY!"

I bolted out these words with power as Reverend Jackson led us into a revolutionary chant. It gave me hope in what was once a hopeless situation. I realized that we were not alone. Hurricane Katrina was now nationally known, and all of our lives really did matter.

When Reverend Jackson marched off the bus, his demeanor meant business. He told us he would ride back to Baton Rouge with us, but then we would need to call our parents to make arrangements from there. Then he said a word of prayer, "Lord, please watch over us as we journey out of the city, be our guide and our light as we make it safely."

When we climbed onto the charter bus, instructors immediately told us to put our heads down in our laps until we got out of the city. We were up against fear of the unknown as the tension and violence were gaining ground in New Orleans. I didn't know what to expect so did what I was told. I quietly rode out of the city into the night and finally made it to Baton Rouge a little bit after midnight. Then I rode with Alana to Houston and flew home to Saint Louis the next day. This was the longest week of my life!

When I got on the plane, I put my hoodie on and fell into a deep sleep until it landed. As I arose out of my seat, tears began to stream down my face. I had no control. Tears came from frustration, sorrow, joy, stress, relief, and comfort. The other passengers witnessed my bursting of emotions from nearby aisles, but I had no shame in displaying what I felt publicly. I was transitioning from a tragedy. I had no luggage, only my phone, and a small tote.

I wandered through the airport to find the exit when a steady hand tapped me on my shoulder twice. It was my dad. I was so thankful to see him again. I lunged into his arms like a toddler for a hug. I couldn't believe how much my life had changed since I saw him just one week ago.

I was hungry and homesick, so we stopped at White Castles. I needed chicken rings and cheese fries to help soothe my soul. After I ate, my dad took me to see my momma. As we pulled up to her driveway, she burst through the doors and ran to hug me. They made sure I had everything I needed to feel comfortable. I mostly needed rest and relaxation. I sat down in my mother's living room and collected myself. Then for the first time, I turned on the television to watch the news coverage. All I could see was devastation. I couldn't believe what was on the news. I learned that my school would be closed for a complete fall semester. I was overwhelmed by this news. I was taken back by all the reports and headlines about New Orleans. I thought to myself, and I was just there! We continually prayed for the people of New Orleans and their transition to safety. At that moment, I realized how grateful I was to have a home and family to come back to. Others were not as fortunate, and my heart ached for them.

The first full day of being home, I woke up from a nap with the worst headache in the world. There was a throbbing and burning sensation in my temple. The stress, uncertainty, lack of food and sleep was all coming down on me. I should have turned my phone off, but I kept it on so I could let my friends and family know that I was ok.

What I thought was the end of the storm was only the beginning. I went through the most depressing time of my life. Although I would enroll in courses at a university not far from home in Saint Louis, I still felt distant from being at peace. Taking baths became a challenge for me. I was frightened to be surrounded by water. It took me back to

Hurricane Katrina.

I would unexpectedly cry at random times throughout the day because the pain would sneak up without warning. It was hard to talk about the high waters, the bodies, and stress. Death seemed to be everywhere, yet people were still trying to survive in New Orleans.

People would always ask me, "What happened?" Every time, I would have to re-live my story repeating it over and over. Inquirers acted like I could tell them in one short sentence. Strangers would want to know what happened in the 1st person. I would ask them, "Do you have an hour?" Whenever I talked about the storm, it scraped off the scars recycling the pain. My headaches would start again. Although I didn't mind sharing my story, it was draining and painful. I needed to be alone. I needed time to grieve by myself so I could heal.

I had to get away. I needed time away from the questions, apart from a new school and regulations, away from speeches, explanations, and expectations. It was in November when I packed a small bag, bought a concert ticket and an accompanying bus ride. Kanye West was on tour for his album, Late Registration. It had come out that fall. Ironically, the album helped me heal and lift my spirits tremendously during that time.

Appropriately titled, I registered late to a new school in the middle of my displacement. Each track related to a different emotion that I was experiencing. The concert was three hours away. I couldn't find anyone available to go with me, so I took a solo trip. That was one of the best concerts of my life!

The tour was amazing because of the sporadic events that happened right before the concert started. It wasn't that late in the evening, but on this chilly night, it was already dark outside. I got off the bus, which dropped me off by the concert tour buses. Since the concert didn't begin for another two hours and the box offices were not opening the lobby doors yet, I knocked on the rear door of the arena by the tour buses. I thought to myself; I'm getting in this building, it's cold out here!

A man opened the door, "Hey there, can I help you?"

"I'm Shanté Berry" I replied. "Ohhh yes, Shanté Berry!!"

He jokingly responded as if he knew who I was.

We both laughed, and he asked if I was there by myself.

I said, "Yep so you should let me inside."

He opened the door and let me inside the backstage venue. There I was...backstage at Kanye's Touch the Sky Tour. I saw familiar faces from television and music walking right past me. It turns out that it was Kanye's cousin, who greeted me at the door. A very charismatic man with an eclectic and exciting tone of voice. He gave me a backstage pass and invited me to hang out until the concert kicked off. We chatted for a bit about my journey over the last few months then he told me that if I wanted to meet Kanye, I could go backstage after the concert.

Moments later, a lady approached me and asked if I needed a massage. I said, "Sure!" She led me over to the massage chair. I felt like I was receiving celebrity treatment.

I came a long way from being locked out of the concert just ten minutes ago. Now I was backstage, networking with artists, and getting a Swedish massage. I planted my face down in the massage chair and the massage therapist relieved multiple knots in my back.

Then I heard a man with a deep voice come up to the chair and started playing with my arm bracelets. Examining my jewelry, he said, "Baller!" With my head held down, I chuckled, and said: "thank you!" I didn't know who that could've been, but the massage felt too great to lift my head to see.

Ten minutes later, I wrapped my massage up, and it was time for the show to begin. The concert was incredible, and the performances were well worth the wait. Each song spoke right to my current situation. When Kanye performed the song, Heard Em' Say, I was personally living what the chorus repeated, "Nothing is ever promised tomorrow, today." I was grateful for the bare essentials and my life.

The song, Crack Music was performed and Kanye said "God, how could you let this happen?" My eyes watered as I thought about a flooded New Orleans. I wasn't blaming God. However, I was frustrated and confused at the lack of timely relief. It contributed to the mass mayhem days after the storm. The response was an injustice to the citizens of New Orleans. Many lives could have been saved with a more adequate and timely response.

When the final song was performed, Touch the Sky I was empowered and enthused about moving on with my life, education, and pursue my dreams further. Better days were ahead of me, which led to Kanye walking right by me as I was backstage. It turns out my bus was leaving in 5 minutes, and I had to decide to either get on the bus or meet one of my favorite rap artists. I had enough experience with being stranded, so I looked out for my best interest and got on the bus to go back home.

Hurricane Katrina taught me valuable lessons in life. Although I was young, I always believed everything happens for a reason. Just because the storm is approaching, it doesn't mean you can't face it, and even if the storm has passed, it doesn't mean it's over. If the sun is shining, you are given another day to live and continue riding out the undercurrent of the storms your life may bring.

In my eyes, life is one continuous storm. Some storms are serene while others are turbulent. Some storms you can see coming and some swoop in swiftly without any warning. It would help if you stayed vigilant and prepared for the next. Although you can't control the storm, I've learned that you can control how you respond to it. When the storm passes, the season in your life should pass as well. You are improved, sturdier, capable, mature and wiser because of it.

Faith, Healing & Forgiveness Fearlessness

Material possessions come and go, but as a survivor, you are blessed with another day to live your best life. Even if you lose faith, there is a path to rebuilding your faith. Jeremiah 29:11 says, "For I know the plans I have for you, plans for you to prosper and not harm you, plans to give you hope and a future, declares the Lord, then you will call on me and come and pray to me, you will seek me and find me when you seek me with all your heart."

Faith is powerful. Faith is having the complete trust and confidence in something or someone. For me, I put my faith in God. Trusting that His plans are better than my own fueled me to go forward regardless of the forecast. Although you may go through stages of depression, displacement, or separation, you cannot let defeat settle into your spirit. The trick of the enemy is to get inside of your thoughts and develop a negative playlist to replay to yourself regularly. "I can't, I won't, and I'm not," are all negative affirmations. You must stop the negative playlist from developing a positive mindset. Transitioning your thoughts and action to words of power and inspiration changes the narrative that you tell yourself. This can ultimately bring you closer to the life goals that you desire.

Faith inspires us not to worry about the storms because God has a divine plan for your life. Your house, car, clothes, and material belongings can all be replaced. The miracle inside of your misery is that you are still alive and breathing to live another day. You can start over and build a new life. If your heart is still beating, you have a purpose. God is a healer and a restorer. He can give you everything that you have lost and more.

Is there is a storm that you are seeking to overcome, but you don't know how to weather it? Storms may not always be physical. There are emotional, financial, internal, health and even invisible storms. How you weather the storm may affect how you live your entire life. Will you give up at the first sign of hardship? Alternatively, will you develop the will power to have faith and keep going?

Accepting where you are is a critical component of healing from a traumatic storm in your life. Where there is a tragedy, there is a loss. Where there is a loss, there is grief. The stages of grief range from denial, anger, depression, and acceptance. I had a significant transformation when I connected with positive and healing sources. This made a considerable difference for me during my storm. I started to speak at different events about what I had seen and endured in New Orleans to encourage and empower others. However, I realized that it may have been too soon for me to talk as I was still depressed.

I would put on my armor during the day to speak then go home and cry at night. When the world moved on to the next big news story, I continued to grieve Hurricane Katrina and sat in that depression. I had to be open to forgiving myself because, for a long time, I blamed myself for what had happened to me. I thought that if I didn't put myself in certain situations in the first place, my life would be completely different. Then I learned that circumstances didn't happen to us; it happens for us. Your storms have a purpose too. Decoding the lesson in your storm is going to allow you to arrive at a turning point in your life that brings you to victory. What season are you better prepared at now to go into? You made it through this, what can't you do?

You can exercise turning your pain into progress. Keeping your mindset healthy and focused during the storm is necessary for healing and development. Embracing the spirit of depression will cause you to be defeated. Some of the most painful times in your life can also be the most progressive. You can use negative energy to push the positive out. Inhale fearlessness, gratitude, confidence, and happiness. Exhale the fear, doubt, depression, and negativity. The sooner you apply this, the quicker you can create room for opportunities to appear. Creating short term goals are an essential part of growth because it gives you attainable and measurable benchmarks that you can achieve every day.

When a traumatic situation happen in life this can create trauma that can remain in our lives if we don't heal. Situational trauma also can involve triggers the effect how you respond emotionally to different situations. Our emotions can be tied to an event, person or place where the trauma happened and those memories can create anxiety, depression, lack of self-esteem, fear, and doubt. It's important to seek professional help when you have those symptoms. Talking through you trauma and healing is a process. It is something that can stay with us and the pain can spill over into every aspect of our lives if we don't heal properly. Don't be ashamed of taking care of your mental health. While your wounds in life are probably not your fault, your healing is your responsibility.

Developing an active prayer life helped me to become genuinely open with God about my heart's desires and worries. I learned that having an active prayer life brought peace, understanding, and restoration to grow. God will not abandon you during the final hour if you trust and seek him first.

When we look beyond the 'now' and get into the 'how' we can become glorious in the storm. God is intentional about blessing you so be deliberate in your actions. Know that God did not give you the spirit of fear. He wants you to be fearless, vibrant, and courageous to go boldly in the direction of your dreams. Once you can understand that, you can look at any significant setback as only a setup for a huge come-back. When your situation gets better, continue to pray and ask God for guidance.

How you define greatness for yourself is a critical part of manifesting it in your life. The textbook definition of greatness defines it as the quality of being great, distinguished, superior or imminent. I define greatness as discovering, developing, and delivering your God-given purpose. Therefore, greatness is much less what you have and more so what you give. What inspires you to jump out of bed in the morning? What ambitions wake you up at night? Are the things that make your eyes light up synonymous with what you are pouring your time into every day?

Where there is a storm, there is water. Where there is water, there can be cleansing. You have the power to allow your storm to cleanse and renew you. You can be set free from any bondage, pain, and turmoil that it may leave. Gain strength in solidarity and working through the stages of grief. The process of healing is never overnight. Overcoming your storm is a process of several things that starts within you. Develop faith amid your situation, possess the fearlessness to keep going, and transform a negative situation into a positive outcome.

Butterfly Effect

"I'll knock you from an amazing grace to a floating opportunity."
-Geneva E. Marshall

A massive earthquake in Los Angeles happens because a butterfly has flapped its wings 21 years ago. A category five hurricane only arrived in this form because that same butterfly has now flapped its wings 28 years prior and an icy blizzard in Saint Louis just happened due to a prior instantaneous small event. These are adapted examples of theories from the butterfly effect.

What does any of this have to do with your world and what does all this mean? Do people wonder if a seemingly minor event in life can result in a significantly different outcome? Since the moment of my existence, I'm sure none of the events that had occurred in my life were bound to happen if I were not alive. I believe there are no coincidences in my world, nor yours. God orchestrated everything to happen for a reason. Before Hurricane Katrina, I had other storms that I had to face as a child. I wasn't aware that they were storms at the time. I thought this is life and I must get through it.

As a child, I felt limitless. I knew it was God telling me that I had an exciting journey ahead. I dreamed of far off places. I remember riding down the street with my dad driving and a sudden feeling of opportunity came upon me. There was an inner voice letting me know that I can see the world and more if only I would first believe it was possible. It all starts with a belief.

When I was fifteen, I told my dad, "Hey dad, I think I've outgrown home. I'm going to move away, ok?" He looked at me with amazement. He was shocked. I knew what I wanted to do at such a young age. We had many car conversations about life in general. My dad never hesitated to lecture his children, especially in the car because you had nowhere else to go making it the best place.

Theoretically speaking, the butterfly effect means that something earlier affects results, direction, and the total physical state of your current situation. More specifically, the peanut butter and jelly sandwich you ate at age seven have a direct result on the red shoes you wear today. The decisions that you made yesterday impact your life ten years from now.

What is the underlying meaning of cause and effect in your life? Do you take responsibility and full ownership of everything that has happened, good or bad? Also, if something happens in your life positive or negative, are you forever changed as a person? Therefore, if you change even the smallest of life's details, can you completely change the outcome?

Do you see this to be true from the situations in your life? If you let the storms no matter how big or small develop the greatness within you, who is responsible? How you handle your difficulties in life make a difference in your growth. You can let adversity be a hindrance or a stepping stone to your success.

People often delight in the beauty of butterflies but are rarely concerned with the changes it has gone through to achieve that beauty. People may admire your physical characteristics or material possessions as if those are the most valuable things you possess. Many times, they are not aware of your journey beyond that physical admiration.

People go through situations, storms, and circumstances that in the end, I know beyond a shadow of a doubt are meant for some to endure. The storm creates and pushes you to a place where you can appreciate the victory even more. I look at the theory of the butterfly effect as a constant reminder of cause & effect, past & present, and journey & discovery.

I've wondered what it would be like to have a simple and normal life. People would tell me about their crystal-clear path to success. I would be highly confused by it. They were raised in a two-parent household with their siblings, went on to ivy league school and graduated summa cum laude, and earned a great job with excellent benefits. Then what happens next? Their high school or college sweetheart proposes and they get married and live life happily ever after. Perfect.

For me, that fantasy life moved far from my mind after age eight. I knew my life would have order, but it wouldn't be perfect. I am surprised when some people expect success, growth, and progress to look the same in every person's life. Aren't you? We have different journeys, and if our paths cross, it doesn't mean that our paths should mirror. I respect an individual's mission and that you have your own story.

As millennials, my older brother and I grew up under the television influence of Alvin and the Chipmunks, Salute Your Shorts, Doug, Family Matters, In Living Color, Hey Arnold, and Martin, to name a few. As far as videogames go, Nintendo and Sega Genesis were our time clock, and we clocked in daily.

My generation was one of the first generations to experience media streaming from the internet into society. I didn't have the social media outlets that children have today. A lot of my activities and hobbies were shaped by old-school development. I played hide-and-seek outside, but I could whoop butt in Street Fighter and Mortal Kombat. I was exposed to my brother's video games that gave me a good balance between the Sega Genesis and my Cabbage Patch dolls. My social life was not defined by how many likes I received on Facebook, but by my personality and character. My only care in the world was if I beat the next level of Super Mario Brothers and how many lives I had left, and of course, school.

My parents kept me balanced with outdoor and social activities. However, it was vital that I had full use of my imagination, creativity, and energy as a child. They gave me an abundance of support and guidance. My brother and I started a business in the third and fourth grade selling candy.

It was called, Berry Kids Candy and my parents would go to Sam's Club and buy in bulk so we could sell candy in our front lawn under the carport. In the sweltering summer heat of Saint Louis, I stood outside for hours to run the candy shop. It was like a lemonade stand but with so much more. From pickles to pretzels, Now-Laters to Snickers, I had everything to fix the neighbors' sweet tooth. I was aware of opportunities and what it would take it to build and accumulate money. Looking back, I admire how much my parents gave of themselves to keep me active and engaged in different endeavors.

My parents met in high school in Saint Louis, MO. They went to college and then moved to California to start a new life. My mom is the strongest woman I have ever known. She has the tenacity for what she wants in life and the willingness to survive the setbacks and start- overs. My mom was an educator working in elementary education to help students excel. My father was 6'3ish. He was much taller than me with brown skin, a huge joyful smile, and slanted eyes. Whenever I would peek into his room, I couldn't tell if his eyes were open or closed. "Daddy, are you sleep?" I would ask. "Nah, I'm just reading suga."

My dad was always reading, and my mother walked to the beat of her own drum. She expected the best, and she made sure I knew that. I felt like she had earned trophies for handing out the best whoopings because she never backed down when the time was right. I was sure my mother took classes for whooping in school since she was so effective and efficient doing it. I thought she was strict, but always fair.

My mother is all of 5'5 with a beautiful smile, almond-shaped eyes, and a curvy figure. She was glamorous, classy, and bossy, but could also be high- strung and assertive when she needed to be. Our temperaments were at different levels 90% of the time, but we balanced each other out most days.

My parents found a powerful church called Mount Zion Missionary Baptist Church, and soon got married. Our pastor at that time, the late Dr. E.V. Hill served as the leader and a giant in the Christian community. He had a worldwide ministry, a relentlessness spirit of giving, and commitment to the community. His compassion for the poor and homeless led him to create initiatives such as "the Lord's Kitchen." This food ministry for the homeless fed countless of people in the Los Angeles community. My family would often go to volunteer on weekends. Even as a young child, I felt our Pastor's impact on the city and the world. Our church family was very close-knit, and we served as a community to uplift and supported each other. When he baptized me at age seven, I was excited about the experience, but I didn't understand its significance until I grew older.

My brother Tony and I were born 18 months apart. He was the oldest. I was a quiet and calm baby while he was the rambunctious one. My parents could leave me alone in the living room with a Cabbage Patch doll, and I would stay put. My brother, on the other hand, would be jumping off the refrigerator! Two entirely different personalities, but my brother was and is my best friend. We were "good as gold" as a loved one called us, and our early childhood was very happy and adventurous. Together, we went to Magic Mountain, Disney Land and had fantastic birthday parties. Although we were not rich, I had love, support, and family.

My dad's business burned down to the ground during the Rodney King Riots in Los Angeles, CA. I remember him walking my brother and I down near Crenshaw Boulevard through the remains of the smoke, fog, and debris. He showed us what used to be his workplace. This was the same place I played at after school, the same area where I ate Jamaican beef patties and drank sparkling lemonade. It was gone. At seven years old, I didn't fully understand the impact that the events had on society and how it would change our lives forever.

The riots started on April 29, 1992, after a trial jury acquitted four L.A.P.D. officers of assault and use of excessive force. Civil unrests were occurring all over the city causing the smoke to rise slowly above Los Angeles. I felt the backlash from the police brutality that was blatantly caught on camera. While the video evidence was displayed in court, it was ignored by an all-white jury in Simi Valley. The video showed a black motorist, Rodney King, being savagely beaten by mostly white police officers.

The demonstrations in L.A. were an awakening of social, political, and racial injustices in America. America had a colorful mask over the underlying problems and the injustices that existed. Community members took the rage to the streets, and it affected my community. The front porches in Southern California became barbecue pits full of flames and of what was. It started in South L.A. and caught like wildfire spreading into other areas.

All of this happened because Los Angeles police officers were videotaped beating a black Rodney King following a high-speed police pursuit. Thousands of people throughout the metropolitan area rioted over six days after the jury's verdict of acquitting the police officers of all charges. As they walked free out of the courtroom, it sparked a violence spree that ended with 3,767 buildings and businesses burned down, 6,345 people arrested, and 44 deaths[i] The uproar was to put a voice against racism. Mr. King was nearly beaten to death by the four police officers using unsubstantiated excessive force. It was tragic.

As a young child, I watched Los Angeles burn down. It was a lot for me to process. I didn't know why my dad's business had nothing, but a frame left to it or how my favorite snack shop next door was now a pile of ashes. I remember the snack shop being Korean-owned, but fire and flames did not discriminate in my community.

As I saw the racial hatred, I knew I was in the wake of a significant event that would change history forever and challenge our maturity as a nation. Race relations in America is as relevant today, and they were then. We can continue to leave our nation naked and untouched as if it doesn't have any infections or we can let our words and conversations start to heal. Having honest conversations about racism can be the medicine to repairing the problems that are still prevalent in our society.

The constant reflection of my seven-year-old self is in a t-shirt saying purchased by my dad at that time that read, "No Justice, No Peace, No Justice, No Peace, and Still No

Justice." While I was too young to process what injustice was, I felt the energy was powerful around me.

Flash forward to 2015, I took the same walk up Crenshaw Boulevard to Leimert Park, but this time to gather in solidarity for the shooting of Mike Brown, an African-American teenager killed by law enforcement in Ferguson, MO. After the L.A. Riots, my family relocated back to Saint Louis.

The smell of fresh cut green grass, cedarwood, sweet pea flowers, and pinecones reminded me of home. Although I was born in L.A., being raised in Saint Louis had a significant impact on me. This is where I would grow to know and love as home sweet home. Saint Louis had unpredictable weather extremes. I experienced everything from tornadoes to twelve inches of snow to heat index advisories. The Gateway Arch downtown towered over the Mississippi River, and it attracted many tourists. I saw it as a statue or representation of home. Wherever I traveled in the world, that shiny sharply designed skyscraper Arch always brought me back home. Ten toes down, I once heard an older relative say, "You works where you work."

Saint Louis is not a stranger to struggle; it has a strong force amongst its people. Growing up in a stable inner-city community with parents that were educators had me surrounded continuously by teachers and community leaders. Some people become comfortable and complacent with struggle, but it was a hard concept for me to grasp. If you're not moving forward and progressing daily, then what purpose are you living for? I realized that I was addicted to progress. The city, itself being a small population had a more substantial feel to it because of the density. I recalled growing up that the town was severely segregated. Lewis and Clark, Natural Bridge, Chuck Berry, Ike, and Tina Turner are some well-known names associated with Saint Louis.

The slow vibe, but fast thinking pace made Saint Louis feel like home was not quite in the north or south, but somewhere in the middle of America. It's known for the best Chinese food, Italian restaurants, Ted Drews, and Midwestern views. The weather was either too hot or too cold and then perfect for at least two weeks in between those times. There is genuinely no place like it.

Saint Louis is the home of the World Series Cardinals. I proudly represented their colors as a symbol of strength and pride in our city. Saint Louis equipped me with the tenacity, persistence, boldness, and steadfast spirit that I needed to survive the storms ahead. The city pushed me follow my dreams. I can't imagine my life without this city and the people.

It may be too much for a newcomer, but in due time, one adapts to the pace and the tone of Saint Louis. It's the type of city that usually keeps someone within its city limits because of external factors that can't be controlled. You could love it, you could hate it, but I couldn't exist without it.

I remember times when I was ready to go, but once gone for a period, I couldn't wait to get back. It's easy to grow comfortable and fall in love with Saint Louis. It branded me for life. I anticipated my return home from college. It felt great to get back to the familiarity of home after being away so long.

A year before I left for college, I was blessed with my first baby brother, Jhaylen. I longed for a younger sibling to influence and care for and here he was. Jay was everything I prayed for in a younger sibling. A cute, cuddly, happy, smart, pie-faced baby boy I nicknamed "porker" because of his bright complexion and the shape of his face when he laughed. Jay went everywhere with me, from the mall to the movies, and even showed up at my high school for surprise visits.

Five years later, another baby brother was born, Jhordan. I became a big sister all over again. Jhordan was the sweetest brown-eyed baby. He reminded me of a Precious Moment's character. It was such a joy to see both of them grow and blossom. Caring for them made me more responsible and opened my heart as they grew into their own. Although my two younger brothers and I have different mothers, it never affected my access to them. I wanted to be there regardless as a source of guidance, support, and love.

My older brother Tony and I initially had a hard time adjusting to Saint Louis. We were the "new kids on the block." We attended elementary school in the Ferguson-Florissant School District. Our new classmates didn't like our California style of clothing and "west coast" accent. As a reserved and conservative little girl, I was the perfect target for bullies. I had huge glasses, and I hadn't hit my growth spurt yet.

In the fourth grade, I began to get bullied. Girls in my class were extremely mean and called me everything from four eyes to frog to beaver. I didn't understand because the same girls would try to be my friend on the school bus or the playground. They never put their hands on me, but the name-calling, teasing, and taunting, was just as worse. It was a show, and I was not too fond of it. I didn't care for drama or conflict, so I ignored the insults and name-calling. I tried to avoid the girls who did this, but it fueled them, even more, to keep up their verbal taunting.

One day things went too far. During lunch, the ring leader of the mean girl pack, Tiana walked over to my lunch tray and grabbed a chicken nugget off my plate. She chewed it up and spat it back on my tray. I was disgusted! That was the final straw. I had tried to play nice, but this was enough, so I snapped. In two seconds, I went from the four-eyed frog to a Power Ranger.

I got off the cafeteria bench seat, picked up the tray, and shoved in Tiana's face. We began to fight and rolled across the cafeteria floor pulling pigtails and throwing fists. It went on for what felt like twenty minutes. It was a horrible scene from the show "Love and Hip-Hop" but with fourth grad-ers. I felt liberated!

The kids started to whisper and snicker around the school, quiet. Shanté can fight. Awwwww shoot. I was tired of being disrespected. That day with Tiana was a crazy day for me. My first fight and first time going to the principal's office. I was a "straight A" honor roll student. What was I doing in the principal's office?

I got suspended. The next day my dad and mom came up to the school to talk to my teachers and the principal. They were proud of me for standing up for myself, but they did not want me fighting every day. I explained to them that the girls had been messing with me for a while. My dad had a chat with me about self-defense and told me,

"Shante, don't let nobody get in your face!"

I took it literally.

For the next few weeks at school, it was like Mortal Kombat on the playground. I had the benefit of having an older brother with plenty of practice fights under my belt. If anybody came close to getting in my face, it was time to fight.

There is a significant difference in being quiet versus reserved or shy versus laid back. Kids didn't know how to read me. They thought I was timid and would not fight back. They were wrong. Boys, girls, tomboys. Whoever tried me was in for a fight. One day, a boy at school approached me on the monkey bars and wouldn't move out the way as I came across. He got too close, what I considered, "in my face" so I dragged him down off the monkey bars with a leg wrap movement and we fought.

While boarding the bus for a field trip, a girl jumped me in line. I didn't have it. Because she was "in my face," I swung on her, and we fought. I never made it on the field trip. I was on a rampage and found myself right back at the principal's office.

My parents had to have another talk with me about my

accumulation of fights and aggressiveness. I didn't understand as I was defending myself and following their directions. I couldn't let anyone disrespect me anymore and get in my face. I had enough!

Then they gave me clarification that they didn't mean "in your face." It was more like if I felt threatened or picked on. I then developed maturity about situations and avoided fights. I toned down my aggression and didn't see the need to fight. However, I didn't tolerate disrespect. Sometimes you can put fear in someone with just a look. They know not to test you. Bullies only test who they think won't fight back. They try to find the person that's different and highlight those differences to belittle them. Bullies usually are the saddest on the inside because they are battling through their insecurities in life.

I think the most important thing for a child to have is a stable domestic upbringing. Fortunately for me, I had two solid parents. My father and mother were an interesting and dynamic combination. My father has always been an honorable father, who put his kids first. Words can't describe his love for me. He made sure I knew the value of education, culture, integrity, and respect. He also equipped me with an appreciation for my heritage and culture. In my discovery of my purpose and position in life, I have seen my dad work hard and sacrifice a lot for my brothers and me.

He built his own business up from nothing. My father served as an educator in the Saint Louis Public School system, mentor, sports coach, and built his own business, an event mobile entertainment service. He took his love of music and entrepreneurship to a different level. My dad started with one speaker and expanded his brand. I saw the spirit of entrepreneurship early in life and understood the value and impact that it could have on my life. I'm appreciative of my dad and what God has blessed me with.

When my parents divorced, my life became complicated. My brother and I went through ten years of custody battles and complications. My dad was granted primary custody, and we were apart from my mother. I would talk to her every day and see her on weekends. This living situation taught me how to be very independent growing up. My hair was also independent. It was a daily project. Thankfully, my dad's sister was a hairdresser. When I was on my own, I mastered the art of making a solid ponytail and could even make bangs now and then.

Unfortunately, I felt like we were used many times as ammunition against the other parent. That's the drawback of having two parents that were very passionate and loving. I regularly experienced a lot of pain in those years, feelings of inadequacy, doubt, fear, rejection, guilt, and sadness followed me. I lost confidence in myself. My home life became unstable and uncertain because I did not know when someone would get mad and who would pop-off. My life was unpredictable. I hated to see my parents fight. It was always a scary situation for me.

I wondered what was worse, having two parents that are always at odds or being raised in a home with an absent parent. I'm sure both scenarios had equally damaging effects on a child. Somehow, I managed to channel those feelings together and translate it into motivation to do better and be positive about the imperfections in my life. I started to pray more and ask for peace and direction. Music helped me develop tranquility, self-love, and confidence.

When my father was asleep, I would explore his cd and cassette collection and pick out albums that I thought were interesting. I sat on my floor in the middle of my room and had a concert. Aretha Franklin, Angie Stone, Lauryn Hill, Chaka Khan, Erykah Badu, and India.Arie were the headliners. I grew to have a strong appreciation for various genres of music. I experienced the impact that had on my spirit and well-being. I learned that just because the music has stopped, it doesn't mean that the message has. Words continue to resonate long after the music has stopped. The right melody and words within a song could hug you softly and start the process of healing.

Adversity for me came at a young age. I knew my parents loved me and were doing the absolute best that they could. Although our home was divided, they validated me. Validation is important. Make sure your children are not the brunts of your frustration and pain. If you strive to make sure your children are dressed well, then you should also make sure your children are equipped internally with love, strength, integrity, and the persistence to rise above obstacles. I knew I had a strong village by the way people from my community poured into my life. Teachers, church family, relatives, and friends became my strong village in a broken home.

God places people in your life for a reason. The day my family moved to San Francisco Avenue on the North side of Saint Louis, I met a lady who would do just that. Mrs. Geneva E. Marshall ran a tight ship at her property on San Francisco. She was a widowed black woman in her late seventies who was very stern, but sweet as well. The apartment downstairs was vacant. Since my family was in a tight spot financially, we were looking for a new place to live. This is how we came to know our new landlord and love her as Granny Marshall. We moved into her vacant apartment the summer before I started 7th grade. My family resided there for over ten years, and we operated like a full-fledged family.

Granny Marshall made sure I knew the rules, and if I got too loud downstairs, she would march her 5'2self down the stairs and say, "What's all that racket going on?" When report card time came, I would show my report card off, and she would tell me, "Now child, you better use your head for something besides a hat rack!!" She would give me $1 for each "A" and say, "Now don't spend it all in one place!"

My fondest memory of Granny Marshall was that she was sharp and focused on her memories. She remembered my birthday, and every year she would surprise me with a tall vase of sweet pea flowers from her garden in the back-yard. I learned the value of a dollar when Granny Marshall made me earned every cent. She would give me money through my hard-earned housework.

Granny Marshall always gave me meaningful tasks around the house such as sweeping and polishing stairs, cleaning out refrigerators, and bleaching down bathrooms.

She ensured that my work ethic was strong. Each task was worth seven dollars. Seven dollars to a twelve-year-old was pocket change to go skating with or perhaps buy a new shirt on sale. I was grateful for the allowance, and I loved that Granny Marshall taught me how to earn a dollar and value it.

Before moving into Mrs. Marshall's apartment, my living situation was rough. My brother and I attended separate middle schools, we had no car, we were residing in a temporary housing unit, and I felt we were one paycheck away from homelessness. I knew that this living condition would not last forever as we were in transition. I believed that better times would come. I walked every day in the brutal Saint Louis winter snow to catch public transportation to school. My dad rode the bus with me, and I was never alone. One night I prayed and asked God to give my dad a car. Less than a month later, we were was blessed with two vehicles.

During this time, I started to realize how important it was to get an education. My dad made it a top priority. Before I made it to the first grade, he was introducing my brother and me to many educational programs, reading books, composing book reports, and engaging in critical thinking and vocabulary exercises. My first big vocabulary word was "aggravated." I used it in a sentence to describe how my brother "aggravated" me. It was perfect preparation for the SAT, ACT, and many other tests to come.

"Nothing comes to a sleeper but a dream! Now wake up Shante!" My dad shouted into the living room.

"It's 7 am daddy! And it's Saturday!" I replied.

I had fallen asleep on the couch watching television the night before.

"I don't care, get up and get your room cleaned and figure out what your plans are for today."

Ugh!!! I planned to rest. I thought to myself.

My dad set the tone for productivity. Laziness was not an option. You need to wake up and go out and make something of yourself regardless of your circumstances. Education was that pathway for me to create opportunities for myself. The school to prison pipeline would never be my future. My father made sure that I wasn't going to become a pipeline statistic. It linked the relationship between black and Latino children, particularly young boys, didn't graduate but go to jail.

Statistics showed that 70% of students involved in school arrests or referred to law enforcement are black and Latino. 68%iv of all males in state and federal prison do not have a high school diploma. The school to prison pipeline is defined as an epidemic that is plaguing schools across the nationii I saw a need for an interruption to this pathway. When incarceration is favored over education, there is an immediate need for change. The implementation of transitional programs, mentorship programs, access to educational opportunities and the reformation of laws to give students a second chance to succeed can be useful. As I saw the educational disproportions in my community, I started involving myself in anything I could to support these changes. As educators, my parents fought against these statistics every day enforcing a proper education as my primary goal.

My life as a teenager was about discovering who I was and surviving to be me. I was flat chested with Coke bottle glasses and an imperfect smile. I had to grow into loving myself just the way I was. In middle school, I met three girls, Princess, Ayuana, and Melissa. I called them my sisters because we were close and looked out for each other. We skated, shopped, bought Christmas & birthday gifts for each other, and genuinely liked and cared for one another.

As sisters, we shared similar family dynamics and growing pains throughout the years. It was vital for me to have those connections in my adolescence. I couldn't imagine going to events and outings without them. Even after our first year of high school when we made other friends and navigated into different directions, we always had sisterly love for each other. This helped me find self-love. It was like looking in a mirror and loving what I see or listen to a track from a music artist and feeling the beauty within.

When I first felt the crisp breeze of winter blowing onto my Gateway Jaguar tracksuit, I knew it something special. Track and field started as something to do after school, but eventually, I began to love what I considered flying in the wind. It was an outlet from everything else.

As long as I was running, I could go into a high on endorphins and be at peace with everything. I was a long-distance runner. When it was time for me to run, I'd imagine my high school crush waiting for me at the end of my final lap. I had to get there! I could run for multiple laps until people forgot about my event. I was consistent, calm, and focused. I let nothing take my focus off of my goals. It's funny how some things that you start doing early in life never leave your spirit. That strong urge remains with me today. Working out is a part of my routine, my life, and a part of my total well-being. I loved my high school. It wasn't perfect, but I had a family there with significant friendships and connections. Most of my teachers and administrators wanted to make a difference. From metal detectors in the morning to crowded and crazy school bus rides in the afternoon, high school was a fast, fun learning experience. I'm glad my father gave me the opportunity to choose where I wanted to go. My school specialized in Science, Math, Engineering, and Technology. My class had so many different personalities and cultures. I loved the diversity and the way we all came to together.

Growing up, I was blessed with many positive influences in my life. My maternal grandmother has over 25 grandchildren including myself. She remembers and finds a way always to make me feel individually unique. Spending time with her and going to her house was a place of peace for me. She was calm to many of my storms. I thank God for her and the presence she had in my life.

My paternal grandmother passed away when I was a baby, but her legacy was reliable and relevant. I often felt like I knew her. I believe she was very much a part of who I am. Cleo Elizabeth Berry had six children, my father being the oldest. Her children carried her legacy of greatness onward. I saw the artistic gifts her children and grandchildren possessed, and it was a real blessing. I wondered if she was still alive, what exactly would she think about me and would she be pleased with how I was living my life. The one thing I desired was physical her presence in my life.

If you don't know your own identity and culture, you can get easily lost in another one. I was raised to honor my ancestors and know my history. I traced my ancestry data back to Sub-Sahara Africa. 84% of my DNA group being represented there. 77% of that group is from West Africa. The countries of Ghana, Nigeria, and Senegal were most likely the subgroups that I belonged to. This meant that I most likely had a grandparent, great- grandparent, or second great-grandparent who was 100% West African. This person would have been born between 1860 and 1920.[iii] I also had DNA from 4 other genetic populations including Native American, North African/Middle Eastern, Southeast Asian, and Northwest European. All this information told a story, my story. It was important that I knew where my ancestors originated from. Why did I have such a large percentage (13%) of European ancestral DNA and no known relatives who were European? To what extent did my ancestors have to endure along the horrific trans-Atlantic slave trade? When did my West African ancestors migrate to Southeast Asia?

My research also showed that if every person living today could trace his or her maternal line back thousands of generations, all of our paths would meet at a single woman who lived in eastern Africa between 150,000 and 200,000 years ago. Though she was one of perhaps thousands of women alive at the time, only the different branches of her haplogroup have survived today. The story of your maternal line begins with her too. That was powerful and fascinating to know.

The Ivory Coast was a busy trading port for the Trans-Atlantic slave trade. Finding out that my family originated from there delighted my soul. For many African-Americans, we had no place of origin that we could connect with and that bothered me. Other cultures could say that their family came from Germany, Spain, or England, yet we were stuck with the southern states before migration. It felt liberating to have a sense of belonging and to know the rich lineage of my history. After my ancestors left the trading port in West Africa, they most likely came through the deep south of Alabama and then migrated up to Missouri. We had the last name of Bean then, which later transitioned into Berry.

I firmly believe our lives could relate to the theories of the butterfly effect. We start as caterpillars trying to find a perfect cocoon to help transition us into adulthood. Some find it early, and some find it late. The good news is that there is a cocoon for each one of us. Once we see that pathway we are ready to transform into a beautiful butterfly. We can become effective in our families, on our jobs, and through our everyday lives. In what ways are you making positive changes in your life? No matter how small, it's a step in the right direction of becoming one less caterpillar and one more effective butterfly.

African myths believe that butterflies are considered powerful symbols of healing, fertility, and other rites. Europeans view the butterfly with great respect and fear because they thought that the human soul took the form of a butterfly, and Chinese and Japanese cultures for centuries see it as a symbol of joy and the essence of happiness. I imagine the butterfly effect includes the beauty of our storms revealing more than a quest to satisfy our impulse to confirm ideas through science. It explains how everything happens for a reason, and that reason is the blueprint of our destiny. Whatever life throws you, catch it! Keep on running and if you hit a curve, swerve and step on the gas!

Pain, Purpose, & Progress

The pain of your past can fuel the purpose of your future. My purpose is rooted in my passion. I'm passionate about helping you live your best life. Spiritually, mentally, emotionally, and physically. Inspiration is a gift that re-gifts the blessings right back to the sender without them even being aware. Discovering your purpose has steps to get there. You must have the courage to unpack your past, heal from your pain and find your passion. Otherwise, you will be living a vicious cycle of pain. I want to help you let go of a life that is cold, guarded, angry and unfulfilled. If that is you, don't allow pain or anger to run your life.

If you're continually cutting people out of your life instead of building relationships and connections that enhance your life, it is time for you to heal and address the source of the pain and anger. While I believe some people are in your life for a season, if you make burning bridges a habit you will eventually start forest fires. It is time to put the forest fires out of your life. You can't get to your purpose if you refuse to look back into your past and heal from situations that hurt you.

If you don't heal, your life will reveal recycled anger, fear, doubt, and sadness. Find a safe space with a confidant or counselor to help you process your difficult life experiences. You cannot heal what you refuse to deal with. Everybody may have an old scar, but if you continue to put a band-aid over a bullet wound, you will not heal properly.

"Riding it out" requires writing it out. Declare your goals by writing them. Make a list of your short term or long-term goals. You are activating greatness in your life. Writing and journaling your thoughts and intentions release an automatic frequency into the universe for beautiful things to occur. This frequency can create an immediate demand with positive results. If you write down a grocery list, those items are most likely to appear within the next few hours in your kitchen. You need and want them, so you make sure you don't forget the items on that list. This is because you are intentional about getting those items.

Are you intentional about living into your purpose? If so, I encourage you to act on it. Writing down your needs and wants will help you acquire your goals. Start today by writing down five short-term goals that you want to get done by the end of the month. Thoughts become things, and when you write them down, you are taking the first step to activate your greatness.

My childhood upbringing was not perfect, but the challenges I had developed my character as a person. You may not have had any control over situations and circumstances from your childhood, but you do control how you respond to them. What I learned from my upbringing, my parents' divorce, being bullied and finding self-love all was a part of my growth and progress.

You will have your good days and bad days, but you can work to remain positive and see more of the good than the bad. Use the painful times of your life to propel you to focus on the positive and let adversity make you stronger. Finding your purpose in life is like finding a place of peace that you can exist. You don't feel obligated or forced, you know it when you feel it. It's effortless, deeply meaningful and delights your soul. It's my happy place that no one can take away from me. The progress that I've made in following my passion and purpose has changed and shaped my life. You have a story to tell. Discover what method you are designed to reveal your story. Will it be through music, art, business or writing? What has shaped you and progressed you to start to move forward in living your best life?

What dreams keep you up at night? If today was your last day on earth what would be your biggest regret? My dream was and still is sharing my writing. Your biggest fear could be your biggest blessing. If you have a dream that won't let you rest, don't ignore it. Do it!

The great motivator and speaker, Les Brown said, "The graveyard is the richest place on earth, because it is here that you will find all the hopes and dreams that were never fulfilled, the books that were never written, the songs that were never sung, the inventions that were never shared, the cures that were never discovered, all because someone was too afraid to take that first step, keep with the problem, or determined to carry out their vision.[iv] Greatness is a choice.

You can choose to labor towards someone else's dream or birth your own.

Southern Comfort

"If you don't understand yourself, you can't understand anybody else."
-Nikki Giovanni

Mardi Gras, magnolias, and miracles. These three things I would soon experience. Growing up in the Midwest and going to college in the South brought many different perspectives and more opportunities for growth. I had experienced New Orleans pre-Hurricane Katrina in a whole new way.

At age seventeen, I stumbled upon my college campus, intimidated, yet filled with anticipation seeking a different world. I saw how college was presented on television, but I didn't know what to expect in reality. The summer air was thick as gumbo, and the clouds hung low enough almost to grab. It was at that moment that New Orleans caught me suddenly and never to let me go.

Even until this day, I have immersed in the culture of New Orleans that it is a part of me. Everything that New Orleans encompassed was strong in spirit. It had a rich history within the gloomy elements of the city. Live oak trees framed the atmosphere and told stories of struggle, sadness, reformation, heritage, and change.

New Orleans was a place that had breathed history, witnessed the Louisiana Purchase, and saw the country grow. It still stood, and I was standing in its streets ready to experience it. I was extremely intrigued by this mysterious city, and I felt fortunate to be able to study, grow, learn, and evolve into an adult here. I was eager to expose myself to every cultural and social experience this beautiful city had to offer. I studied and researched this exciting place that I would call my new home.

The Louisiana Purchase in 1803 caused the city to multiply with influxes of Americans, Africans, French, Creoles, Irish, and Germans. Major commodity crops of sugar and cotton were cultivated with slave labor on large plantations outside the city.

The plantation houses were unreal to me as I had only seen them in movies. After conducting research, I grew enamored mainly by the ways and the people of the south. I respected the elements of the city and the citizens who defined it. My school represented a historic landmark of educational excellence beaming with pride and passion for greatness. It was a perfect fit for me.

I would check out my school's library video database and look at historical documentaries for hours at the beginning of the semester when my workload was not heavy. Being from the Midwest, it was a familiar, yet different tone and pace. The richness of the culture took me by surprise. I never knew of a world like this. I was eager to learn and grow at seventeen. When I arrived in the south, I knew instantly that I was of the south.

The aroma of freshly baked beignets tossed in pow-dered sugar drifted through the humid breezes of the French Quarters. When you bite into a French donut, it was like having a fancy fluffy funnel cake packaged into a neatly breaded donut melt in your mouth. Tasting New Orleans gumbo for the first time was quite the experience as well. Eating the right gumbo was like walking into a party that you knew nothing about, but all of your friends were there. The warmth, flavor, spice, and surprise became incredibly addicting. My surprise was served in the form of a crab leg! I was delighted because this proved that not all gumbo is created equal.

Bourbon Street was a maze of drunkenness, festival, fun, food, music, dancing, and street walking. It was deco-rated in hues of purple, green, and gold. The Mardi Gras vibrancy of colors was symbolic to only New Orleans. Pur-ple represented justice, green represented faith, and the gold represented power. The pungent aroma of piss and beer smacked you in the face right upon arrival on the street. Then moments later, you were immune to it and taken in by the sights and sound. Occasionally, my colleagues and I would roam the French Quarters out of boredom and lack of Saturday activities, only to be drawn back to Bourbon Street like a magnet. I wandered on in awe of so many things going on at the same time. It was an adult playground. For many of us, barely out of our teens, all we could do is look and wonder what all the fun was about. From beignets to broiling hot gumbo that was seasoned to perfection, the food of New Orleans was in a class of its own. The allure of the French quarters kept me coming back.

I wouldn't trade my collegiate experience for any in the world. I had the best learning, cultural, and social experience possible. Are there things that I wish I had done differently while I was there? Absolutely! But that goes with any learning experience. The first time I was taught to eat crawfish, it was a lesson. It took me fifteen minutes to crack the shell of my first one, but by the third try, I had it down. I was in the south, and the south knew how to eat, dance, and enjoy life.

Although this was my first time in the state of Louisiana, it seemed very familiar. The new freshman year brought many opportunities for me. It was a bit overwhelming and daunting at times, but I managed myself well. My classmates came to such a diversity of beauty. Some girls had hair that was twice as long as mine or had different skin tones, hair textures, accents, and body types. It was a beautiful experience to see different expressions of African-American beauty.

Colorism was a harsh reality. It was painful initially. However, I never let it affect my collegiate experience. Thankfully, I was validated at home, so I never felt inferior or invisible. I continued to carry myself as the queen I was raised to be. I remembered flashbacks of my mom randomly complimenting me and telling me I'm beautiful or my dad continuously treating me like a precious diamond, protected, and valued. They thought I was beautiful first and their word was golden.

Colorism started to become a deep concern for me because it affected relationships and the way people treated one another. People from every culture continue to this day to use skin color discrimination to rank beauty, masculinity, social status, and character. It was shocking and somewhat sickening to experience that for the first time in college.

I defined colorism as a confused state of mind that places judgments and assumptions on people based on their skin color. This goes back to slavery where the division of mixed black people and unmixed started — House Negro vs. Field Negro.

This same slave mentality runs deep in our relationships. People develop "preferences" based on skin color and place judgments on people without even knowing them. People can also develop light skin supremacy because they are of a brighter complexion. I was watching Oprah's Life Class one day that had a segment where they covered colorism. They revealed how both darker skin and lighter skin women and men face extreme discrimination in society.

I found myself in a situation that baffled me. I never focused on my skin color growing up. I had rich caramel brown skin complexion like my parents. It was during my freshman year at school when an interaction with a colleague made it clear that he focused on that. In history class, I became acquainted with a guy who had lighter skin. We were in the same study group. He approached me and casually commented,

"Shante you're pretty for a dark-skinned girl. I bet you don't hear that too often, huh?"

I immediately became agitated. I didn't know whether

to ignore his ignorance or let him have a lecture I was brewing up for him. So, I decided on the latter.

"Paul, I find your backhanded compliment offensive. What makes you think that lighter complexion is more attractive and that darker complexion is synonymous with unattractive? Don't try to rank the color of my skin. That's discriminatory, and it's disgusting that you think like that. I don't need your compliments to know that I'm beautiful."

He stared at me in a calm matter as if, to say, "really?"

Then Paul pulled out a brown paper bag out of his backpack with a smirk on his face. "Well if you're not lighter than this bag, you're considered dark skinned, and you'll rank second as far as looks."

"And you rank dumb," I interjected.

"Now get out of my face and don't bring that self- hating logic around me."

I snatched the paper bag from him, balled it up and dunked it in a nearby trash can. He shrugged and walked away surprised that I was offended. That was the first time I experienced someone of my race present that horrible train of thought to me. It was ignorance on another level.

The next day, I saw Paul getting dropped off at school by a middle-aged chocolate skinned woman that looked like she could've been his mom. I wondered did he feel the same way about her? Or worse, I wondered did she condition him to think that way? If a culture of people has been conditioned to hate their skin, most likely they will pass this hate and conditioning down to their children. They will tell their son, "lighter girls are more pretty"; or they will tell their dark-skinned daughter to date a light-skinned man in hopes of having fair-skinned children. This conditioning sickens the self-esteem and relationship that men and woman develop toward their skin color.

Paul's comments were a direct reflection of his conditioning either from home, school, or maybe even the media. Nobody taught him that beauty is skin deep ranging from the deepest chocolate brown to vanilla. There is no rank when it comes to complexion.

A few months later, I met a super sweet and smart girl from Nigeria named Nia. We had a lot of classes together. We clicked and hung out often. She had the richest dark brown skin that was strikingly beautiful, clear, and evenly moisturized. I always complimented her and asked what skin products she used. Nia would shrug off my comments and say, "Just soap and water."

As we got older we lost contact somewhat because of our different majors. We reconnected for lunch in our junior year, and I noticed her skin looked different. It seemed irritated, discolored, and bleached! I was shocked. I asked her if she was doing okay. Nia said she was stressed because of finals. I didn't want to accuse her of bleaching her skin. I know finals can be stressful, but for your skin color to change? I figured something else was going on. Could Nia have run into Paul or someone with Paul's same mentality to make her feel unattractive because of her darker complexion? Nia didn't have the confidence to stand up for herself or better yet respect herself.

I realized there is not a quick fix to end colorism. It is a strong society-ill, but people should start by checking themselves and questioning why they make certain decisions based on preferences. Perhaps they may find themselves misled, uninformed, and fueled to project hatred on a person that could change their life. A friendship, relationship or network vaporizes because someone thinks that their skin complexion is more valued than the other. I learned that colorism exists not only in the African-American community, but Asian, Hispanic, West Indian, and different cultures as well. I began to see it as was a worldwide cultural sickness, not only prevalent in America.

There is a need to search deeply to define why people's preferences are as they are. When you know and love who you are it's hard to stomach another person's self-hate. All you want to do is hope that they see the beauty in themselves and others and stop spreading their internal pain around.

After my first full month of college, I settled in more and was a lot more comfortable in my environment. I felt as if I was there to thrive and the friends that I would make would be attracted to me because of my character and spirit, not by things like skin color or hair texture. I thank God for my uniqueness and my ability to embrace myself completely early on in life. I can see how easily one person's identity can get lost in another's. The standards of superiority that we give our brother or sister based on superficial elements were disappointing.

I came to know New Orleans as my second home. I learned to be sufficient and survive on my own. It was a big task for an eighteen-year-old. I had to pry away from my parents and make my own decisions that would profoundly impact my future. Decisions such as my major, my minor, study habits, my choice of friends, and the people I dated. All these decisions will impact your collegiate career and your life.

It seemed like my image in college was completely different from that in high school. It was now magnified. My parents gave me everything that I needed to succeed. I knew how to focus less on the frivolous things and more on advancing my life toward a bright future. My dad was strict and stern when it came to education, but also fair. I could see why he pushed me so hard.

In high school, I maintained a highly interactive academic and social life, which gave me the great ability to platform, grow, blossom, and network. However, being active in different organization and academics, I lost time for my friends & extracurricular activities. While I had several close friends, I had less leisure time. I focused my energy on scholarships and picking the right college. This wasn't a bad thing because my dedication proved profitable. I made it to my first-college choice. College was the most exciting time of my life thus far. When I made my education my primary priority, I created endless opportunities.

In my college years, I set out to obtain a better balance with my social and academic life. I let social activities develop naturally. I established a network of friends from all over the world. My network expanded from Nigeria, Japan,

Haiti, Virgin Islands, Canada, Boston, New York, and Hawaii – places that I never thought I would be able to discover. Now, I had friends and colleagues who represented a direct connection to various countries, cultures, and lifestyles. I became very active in social groups so I could become more fluid in social settings, networking, and building individual friendships.

The most beautiful thing about my school is that there was a bold sense of legacy, community, family, and excellence the moment you stepped on campus. No matter what individualized clique I belonged to, I represented something big. I represented a legacy of excellence. The administration, deans, and dorm mothers welcomed you with an expectancy of greatness. From that fall onward, I knew I was a part of a profound, rich legacy that future generations would look up to and remember. I knew that my ancestors would have been proud of me for being here.

I explored New Orleans in all of its glory. Every time I would drive over Lake Ponchartrain, just 15 miles outside of the city, I blasted my New Orleans bounce music creating the most an amazing experience. Every year, Mardi Gras became a vast celebration of life, culture, and community. I didn't realize how significant it was to the city or that it was related to a religious holiday. Mardi Gras was "Fat Tuesday," Ash Wednesday was "Lent" and Easter was "Resurrection." They were all closely connected.

Carnival was a celebration of life. The Lent season started the day of fasting, and Easter represented the Resurrection of Jesus Christ. Lent was seven weeks before

Easter like clockwork. There was much to learn and observe. Fat Tuesday guaranteed a one-week mid-semester break. I was always in anticipation of that.

The first time I went to Mardi Gras, I was enamored by the transformation of the city's vibrancy. New Orleans shut down for the parades. The parade floats were as tall as buildings and the beads from the floats were as big as Boa snakes. Contrary to the rumors, you did not need to show body parts to get beads. You just needed to be present and a pleasant participant of the festivities.

The warmth of the people gave me the most joy as well. Anytime you can strike up a meaningful conversation with a stranger; you are in the right place. I gained 15-20 pounds soon as school started. This became known as the "freshman fifteen" because it was a common occurrence for the changes freshmen go through and how our bodies adapted. The cafeteria served its full purpose. Music, food, dancing, fashion shows, laughter, and the events were in abundance.

On Fridays, there was a huge sense of accomplishment that I made it through a long study week. I also knew that the catfish, cornbread, gumbo, and macaroni & cheese waited on me with open arms. My weight climb was now over 140 pounds with way more hips and thighs than I had several months ago. I was a young woman developing, in her own way, at her own pace, and I was completely fine with that.

Change your major, prepare to change your life. I wish my dad would've made those words stick like glue to my forehead. I changed my major countless times. I was interested in and intrigued by everything. Naturally, I am full of wonder, but I knew that if I wanted to graduate timely, then I must focus and decide. I love learning, and I am a lifelong student. My dad was direct and relevant with his concern about me changing my major from biology to business, to psychology, back to biology and then finally business. Indecision got the best of my time and energy.

Initially, I didn't see the big deal since I had an interest in a variety of different majors. There was much that I wanted to learn. I was young and impressionable. That was like taking me to a buffet and then instructing me to get one item or allowing me to have a library card but only read one book. It was absolute torture for a curious mind like mine. I wanted to adventure into a variety of choices until I found confidence in my decision. Changing my major so many times was bold and crazy, but I assured my dad that I would be okay.

Shortly after I graduated, I learned how important it was to follow my heart and never turn my back on my first passion. The same passion that brought me forward would I return to. In hindsight, the best thing would've been, to be honest with me and start college as undecided. At 18, I could hardly make up my mind of what shoes to wear let alone what profession I wanted to be in for the rest of my life.

Going from science to business was risky. The business field didn't initially challenge me the way science did, but changing my major and atmosphere presented more business opportunities, and I loved it! I was a free thinker. I allowed my thoughts to lead me to where I needed to go. My school opened doors for me to be a success in whatever major I decided. When graduation drew near, I had an abundance of opportunities and choices in the field of business, sales, marketing, and journalism.

I was given a great social, cultural, and academic experience all rolled-up into one. The school allowed my dream to come true by attending a higher learning institution and becoming nurtured with the tools to thrive for four years with continued success. It was a blessing to go through those years and walk across the Superdome on graduation day seeing my family waving in the crowd.

I had made them proud, but my proudest day as a senior was when I got my final report card. It had a long list of A's and was my hardest semester ever. I took nearly twenty-two credit hours to catch up with the semester post-Katrina to graduate. I can't recall exactly how I did it, but I remembered I was focused. I finished my last semester strong while working 20 hours a week at Whole Foods Market. Changing my majors threw me off track, and Hurricane Katrina only made things worse. I was far off my roadmap for graduating on time, but I worked hard. Once I saw my uploaded grades for my final semester, I cried tears of joy! I had been through so much as a college student, but it was all worth the journey.

Historically Black Colleges and Universities ("HBCU") hold a special place in my heart. They are institutions of learning that empower people of color to obtain something that was once forbidden and unattainable. They are historic landmarks that should never be underestimated or devalued. Education is precious and it is, such an honor to be a part of that culture.

With 107 HBCU's across the nation, the educational experiences were unlike any other. The campus had a long legacy of family-oriented energy, filled with school pride. My education is priceless. No one can take it away from me. It is a gift and a privilege to have. I value my education so much because I know my ancestors were not given the same opportunity to be free to learn, read, and write, and think for themselves. I had become their dream. What excuse do I have not to wake up and give 110% of my effort toward becoming a success?

After Hurricane Katrina, I returned to New Orleans when our school re-opened in January 2016. I was both amazed and proud of our university President, staff, and faculty for their efforts on reconstructing the campus so that the students could return. The campus was under 6 feet of water for weeks after the storm. There were thousands of dollars in damages, yet we were able to return and finish what we started. It was a miracle!

My school added an extra semester in the summer. I became as engaged as I could and addressed the problems that the city faced. I participated in the National Civic Works initiative as a volunteer. It was called "Louisiana Winter." The group brought together college students nationwide to help develop solutions in the wake of the aftermath. We met with community leaders, the ninth-ward homeowner's association, pastors, and connected with the needs of the community. If they needed a voice, we wanted to be that for them. Hurricane Katrina brought infrastructural, economic, social- economic, and emotional displacement.

Our student group promoted the Gulf Coast Civic Works project. The project sought to bring 100,000 career-oriented jobs to Katrina-effected communities throughout the Gulf Coast with the intent to reinvigorate neighborhoods by building housing, schools, hospitals, and roads. We hosted town hall meetings at Gulfport, MS and New Orleans, LA, where residents discussed the Gulf Coast Civic Works Project and shared ideas and input. Concerns with wages, work training, temporary housing, the building of schools, the distribution of the jobs, and other issues were some of the significant concerns that were discussed. It was overwhelming to see all the work that needed to be done. I was glad to be able to be on the ground and assist with whatever I could for the restoration of the city.

When graduation finally came, it was nothing short of pure joy. After four and a half long years, it brought me to this very day. The beautiful combination of the crisp breeze and the sunny spring weather felt perfect. It created a filter of joy over my entire day.

Truckloads of my family and friends pulled up to the "Big Easy." They came from Saint Louis, New York, Florida and California. I loved that we were together deep in New Orleans. It was such an enlightening and engaging time for me as we toured the ninth ward, ate amazingly good food, socialized, and celebrated our victories. It was indeed a special time.

At that moment, I felt that we were all victorious. It took more than myself to get through those tumultuous college years; it took a village. My march across the stage was highly anticipated, and long sought after prayers, God's grace, vigilance, focus, determination, peace, faith, wisdom, and dedication had helped make this dream come true. It was a miracle. I made it!

Culture, Courage, & Commitment

Every culture has beauty within it. That is what makes beauty diverse and interesting. Loving yourself and loving one another should not be a crime. Honoring your ancestors and those that have paved the way for you is a beautiful celebration of life. Having the courage to live your truth and to love your skin and features even when society may try to make you feel inferior is powerful. God did not make a mistake when he created you! Learning to love yourself is a journey. We have influences in society that tell us beauty has a one-dimensional look. You must know that you are where the beautiful begins. Beauty shines from the inside out so if you take care of your mind, body, and soul you can't stop your beauty from glowing.

Attending a historically black college, graduating, and walking across the stage in spite of my hardships and challenges took courage and commitment. I wanted to accomplish something that I knew my ancestors could have only dreamed of. Graduating from an HBCU nurtured my spirit and put me in an environment for growth, learning, discipline and building lifelong connections and friendships. Education is a lifelong commitment because it doesn't stop when you have walked across the stage. I loved the institution that I graduated from because they were passionate about executing excellence, leaving a legacy, and developing character. No one can take your education away from you. It is essential that you position yourself in an environment that promotes greatness.

College showed me that you should never let age put limitations on your goals. You are never too young or too old to accomplish your goals. When you place limitations on yourself, you delay your progress, and you discourage yourself. If you start college when you are 25 rather than 18, it is fine. Time will pass regardless, and you will continue to mature. Get into the habit of believing that your goals are possible and move boldly in the direction of your dreams without hesitation.

The value of obtaining a higher education can provide more options and opportunities to be successful. No matter what obstacles you may think stand in your way, you possess the power to overcome them. It's critical not to let money, time, or other expectations keep you from developing and furthering your education.

There are endless educational resources designed to help you succeed in higher education. It takes the willpower to search for them and the courage to believe that it is possible. Finding the courage to love yourself and be yourself is all you need to start with. Discover what you are passionate about and where you excel or better yet, how you can dominate in your chosen field. You may not have your destination entirely figured out but directing yourself to a path that can help get you there is essential for living into your greatness. Education is the vehicle to opening many doors for growth, wealth, and advancement in life.

Change is not always comfortable but change usually signifies growth. Don't stay stuck in a familiar place, instead elevate yourself in a new direction. To move towards greatness, you must become comfortable with being uncomfortable at times. The moments when I became extremely frustrated and uncomfortable, I grew the most. I made a significant change so that I could better my surroundings and progress to a higher calling.

I've had seasons where I endured hardships for a reason. Develop the grit to commit to the promises that you have made to yourself. Being a man or woman of your word includes honoring your own word to yourself. You are not exempt from your commitments, especially to yourself. Learn to honor yourself and your word by achieving your dream even if it looks a little different from where you started. What area of your life honors your commitment to yourself? What have you started but do not find yourself finishing? Discover what those things are, search for a reason why you have not completed, and develop a plan to overcome that obstacle.

I have established a system to help me execute my commitments originating from the word PLAN. Prepare, Lead,

Act, and make No Excuses. Prepare for your responsibility by educating yourself about everything that needs to be done to accomplish your goals. Lead by taking initiative and stepping out of your comfort zone to follow through. If you have to introduce yourself to a new person that can potentially help you execute your task, make it a priority. To act is taking specific and reasonable action in accomplishing your end goal. Lastly, don't make room for excuses. Excuses are reasons that you settle to be mediocre. Any excuse that you create sidetracks you from your commitment. It is not worth the dissatisfaction of being stagnant. If you make it a habit of not following through on your commitments, you further disappoint yourself.

Commitment requires consistency, dedication, and consciousness. If you are not focused and conscious as to what you're doing, how could you be committed to it? Some days you may not have all of the answers, but if you can stay committed to the process of learning and developing, you will arrive there. When obstacles come your way, you must refocus, be consistent, committed and conscious about your end goal. The only thing that stands in the way of you reaching greatness is the level of commitment you are willing to put forth. commitment you are willing to put forth.

The Blind Side

"We are only as blind as we want to be."
~ **Maya Angelou**

Young lady, can you please step out of the car and put your hands behind your back?" The officer demanded.

I was in total and complete shock. How did I go from furniture shopping to seconds from being arrested? I was in a new city with a new job, and I was scared. I didn't want to make any sudden movements because I didn't know what the officer's agenda was.

An hour ago, I felt like the luckiest girl on earth. I had a fresh start in a new town. I felt blessed to be selected for a national leadership development program at one of the country's top banks. I was chosen while finishing up my senior year of college. My salary was terrific, life was great, and my hard work was finally paying off.

After picking up my new apartment furniture, I drove through a well-populated college campus area. Moments later, I heard a loud police siren, and I froze. The next few minutes put me in an unexpected position.

The police officer walked to my car, "Do you know what I am pulling you over for?"

"No officer, I do not." I calmly replied.

"You were speeding five miles over the speed limit in a school-zone area."

I was puzzled. I was driving slowly to my destination because I had a car full of furniture. He asked me for my license, registration, and insurance. I gave it to him. Then he noticed that my license plate was from Missouri and declared it invalid in the state of Arizona. I explained to him that I just moved to Phoenix. I was on my way home and then going to work. He didn't budge.

The police officer asked me if I had a piece of mail with my current address on it. I reiterated that I had moved to the city less than a week ago, so I didn't have that information. Walking back to his car, the police officer returned only moments later to ask me to get out and sit on the curb. I did, but I wondered what was going on. The next thing I knew, he placed handcuffs on my wrists and read me my rights. I was startled.

I could not believe what was happening to me!

Then confusion and frustration set in. I almost wanted to tear up, but I showed no emotion. I knew this police officer was over-the-top, excessive, and petty for arresting me. His reasoning was absurd.

Was my Chevy Malibu or I that much of a threat to the community? I sat in the back of the police car pissed off! I never anticipated that I would ever get arrested. I was a high-achieving recent college graduate with a spotless track record. I was a focused, no-nonsense, career woman trying to progress. However, none of that mattered. I wasn't being judged for my character; instead, I felt this was racial profiling. I had never felt so unprotected and misrepresented in my life. The police officer's tone was stiff and unforgiving.

Nevertheless, I remained calm and compliant. I put on my big girl shoes, obeyed the police officer, and got in the back of the police car. I prayed for this to be over! When I arrived at the detainment center, I went through the check-in process. The security guard couldn't run her fingers through my small afro, so she had me take off my elastic headband, and detail searched my puffy black hair. It was strange to be searched and examined like an animal. I didn't want random people putting their hands in my hair. It violated me.

Then I was asked what I did for a living. I replied telling the security personnel precisely what I did. They laughed in disbelief, "You little black girl. A manager? Bank? Ha-ha!"

What they didn't know was that I was telling the truth. I was a rising mid-level manager at one of the top banks in the nation. That still didn't matter. It didn't help me from having to wait in a lightly populated cell for an hour before I was able to bail myself out with my own money. Seven hundred dollars later, I was free and on my way to work. Being detained for not having an in-state license and a piece of paper with my address on it was a pathetic waste of time. It was a disgusting law that helped the police officer have full reign to discriminate against anyone at will. To this day, I don't believe he was justified in arresting me. Instead, I felt preyed on.

Once I could, I called my cousin to pick me up from the

detainment center. He took me back to my car, and I drove to work as nothing happened. I didn't say anything to my co-workers because I didn't want to be vilified. How could they even relate to the way I was treated?

"Well, what happened to you? Why are you late?

What did you do?" They would asked.

I was not in the mood to deal with that. Instead, I was quiet the whole day and reflected on what I had endured. When I got off work that evening, I called one of my good friends who lived on the east coast and told her what happened. She listened to my frustrations and prayed with me to have a better day and a much better week.

The next day, I got an attorney. My attorney worked to get the violations dropped. Three months later, the city of Phoenix sent me a check in the mail for the bail amount that I paid. While I weathered this storm, I know that someone who shares my shade of complexion is struggling to ride it out somewhere.

At the tender age of 22, I had to go through being racially profiled and arrested. It was humiliating, yet humbling. I couldn't help, but think that if my skin was lighter, my hair was blonde, and my eyes were blue that I would not have had to experience this predicament. The bail money wasn't worth my dignity, humiliation, and the disgust that I suffered. I should have never been exposed to such a cruel environment. I didn't want to tolerate it! I was ready to leave Arizona before I even started.

This situation inspired me to be more alert, aware, and sensitive to stereotypes. Does my skin color make people automatically feel threatened, scared, aggressive or negative? Why do people continue to perpetuate stereotypes and make accusations based on isolated experiences? It was wrong. Even though I believed my experience was excessive, I could not live my life getting mad whenever I saw a police officer. What happened to me was unfair and unjust although I couldn't let that victimize me or have any power in my life.

I wasn't alone. In some cases, other black women and men across the country did not make it back home. Like me, they were arrested for a traffic stop or like targeted because of their skin color. I believe that racism and hate can be cured. Only love can heal hate. Mix with therapy, communication, and understanding. Racism is a poisonous energy that targets an oppressed group. I think it's perfectly fine to see color. My color connects me to my culture. A culture that may be vastly different or the same as yours. It's healthy to see color, but filtering color to inject prejudice and claim superiority of lighter or darker skin is not. We should embrace shades of every skin color and generate respect on an individual basis. The denial of seeing color only blinds the long-term effects of racism.

Mike Brown was a human being, not an animal. He was an African-American 18-year-old male, who was fatally shot by a white police officer from an overly- aggressive standoff of surrender. Trayvon Martin, a 17- year-old black boy, did not have to die from bullet wounds inflicted by a neighborhood watch volunteer with a gun. The injustices of his death shook the United States into a state of shock. There are countless African-Americans, particularly young black men who have died unnecessary deaths at the hands of law enforcement fueled by racial discrimination. I believe every person regardless of skin color has a purpose. However, the injustices against African-Americans cannot be overlooked or ignored.

In my opinion, America's ugliest scar is marked with racism. It has been ripped off oozing out blood covering the entire country. I am sick to my stomach with disgust about these tragic cases and others like them. There's a tremendous threat to society, and it's violating the personal safety of my brothers and sisters. Transformation starts with reformation. You have the power to change laws, practices, and policies on these issues. Every citizen has the right to vote. Please vote! You can help save the lives of unarmed men, women, and children fight against the continuous hatred that plagues America today. Stand with me in solidarity and making a difference to make our world a better a place for everyone.

As I write this book, another unarmed person of color is being assaulted with excessive force. Incidents are occurring in real-time throughout the nation. These events are seen on Facebook, the news, and in the newspaper. The media is outraged with the outrage. What can be done? You may march or make a few emotional posts on Instagram, but it seems that everyone then "moves on" living their lives. It's hard for me to move on or find peace when children in our communities are being murdered.

I started to recognize the war going on, the one that

lives inside every person. It's a war of the soul, where differences are picked apart for torturous reasons. It happens when you compare yourself to strangers or get bullied on the internet. Your spirit is broken, and this is an on-going spiritual war that no one wins. When will we ever commune together for the benefit of the human race? Imagine how much further you or I could be in society when egos are set aside, and differences are respected.

Let's try by embracing each other's heritage and getting to know people for who they indeed are — searching the core within means going underneath the skin. You can begin by honoring their character, mindset, expression, sense of humor, gifts, and talents. These are the things hardly experienced because blind eyes shield identities. Don't allow differences to scare you! America was built on the equivalent foundation. In order to move forward, Americans must bridge the generational and racial gaps, and move onward.

Poverty is a disease. It continues to plague communities, races, and people every day. You get an infection first, then you try to catch it in its early stages and more than likely it spreads rapidly in a short amount of time. Opportunists make millions polluting the country by inflicting pain and hatred. It falls heavy on hardworking people, and they are waiting for the day when their struggles will be over. It's hard to believe that institutional systems are set up to perpetuate the problem. It's designed to never see an end to impoverished people, hard times, struggles, and misfortunes. The disease is a cycle of brokenness with a crippling effect. Everyone seems to be screaming for help, but nobody can hear because they are screaming too. As soon as the screaming dies down, another virus strikes. This time it is more lethal and deadly than the first. It gets worse with every cycle.

I've had first-hand experience with a front-row seat living in poverty. My family, friends, and I have had recurring disadvantages that spiraled out of control. These misfortunes appeared to be waiting on us, but we weathered the storms. My only sense of peace and sanity during a complicated world was and still is God. If you can't find God, you may discover the worst alternative. Don't search for a dysfunctional outlet to escape your reality such as drugs, sex or violence. Stop and seek God within. He will give you peace and strength to ride it out. How can you stand firm in your savings, investments, bargaining ability, and buying power if you can't escape your living paycheck-to-paycheck habits?

This kind of financial lack in poor and impoverished communities has been primarily caused by the institutional formula of social engineering and systematic racism. What can create wealth? Opportunities. Communities can't grow or advance without opportunities. The solution to attaining wealth has opportunities. Success has a lot to do with access to opportunity. If there is no access, then the path to success looks distant. Access to education, credit, and housing is critical. Economic empowerment begins with reversing miseducation and affording access to opportunities for success. Disconnecting from televisions and phones to connect to education and empowering sources such as books and discussions are vital to your financial security and livelihood.

As a young girl, I loved having options when it came to my hair. However, I promised myself never to let my hair be a defining ingredient of what makes me feel beautiful. Beauty comes from within and shines outward from there. When you love and nurture yourself while respecting the body God has given you, your true beauty blossoms.

To come to self-love and acceptance, you must swear off the language that comes from hurt and pain. Terms like "bad hair" or "good hair" should be blasphemous. It's self-damaging, and the contextual meaning behind it is wrong in many ways. I call it the "commercialization of self-hatred." This is where racially charged societies convince you that there is something wrong with your natural self to make billions selling your products to "fix it."

Through the acquisition of self-knowledge, you can learn to love yourself unconditionally in your own natural beauty. It would help if you starved the monster who makes you believe you are not good enough and convinces you that you need whatever it's selling. For example, harsh chemical products are usually not good for you. It would be best if you did not let anyone tell you that you need a product to be attractive. You are beautiful just as you are! I love to change my hairstyles often.

Sometimes I want extensions and weaves to achieve certain styles. However, I can separate it from being an enhancement versus dependence. It is a place of understanding where I can look myself and say, "Weave, wigs, and

perms do not make me feel beautiful. I'm already beautiful."
If I choose to enhance my hairstyle with these optional add-
ons, it will not be at the detriment of my hair health. Don't
sacrifice the long- term health of your hair for a short-time
beauty fix.

My transition to being natural had many challenges. My
mother even made discouraging comments about my hair
when I first went natural at age 20. I had just finished washing, conditioning, and combing out my hair. Then I let it air
dry for a second and slicked my edges back. I secured my
hair with a band around my head to form a nice neat afro-
puff. On my way out the door, my mother asked,

"So what are you going you doing with your hair?" I
look at her shockingly and replied,

"It is done, mother. What's wrong with my hair?"

I felt like the sight of my hair disgusted her. It wasn't a
good feeling to know that my mother didn't like what grew
out of my scalp. She was used to the presentation of my
straight hair. I'm sure she perceived my natural hair as being
un-kept, but I didn't let her attitude affect my love for my
hair! I saw her resisting my new natural hairstyle. I knew that
it was only because of my mom's lack of knowledge and
awareness about natural hair. Today, my mom defines her
beauty by being natural. Her hair is now 100% natural and
chemical free. It's up to you to take back, reclaim, and define
your natural beauty.

During my college years, I was in a constant state of
confusion with my hair. I would hear how men love women
that are "natural" with no weaves, yet whenever a woman

got a pattern, most men seemed to find her the MOST attractive! Some men desired straight long hair. While they desired it the most, they wanted it to grow naturally. It was as if I was expected to be something that I wasn't…all while being natural. It's so crazy how some men are conditioned to think. I didn't let the preferences of a few men influence my level of love and acceptance of my natural hair.

Your external identity is just the surface. The real substance of your character is what's within internally. It requires constant upkeep and self-care. If you can pay an extra $300 dollars for a new weave, you can spend an extra $15 on purchasing the right foods. What matters is that your body is getting the proper nourishment to be healthy. I encourage you to start consuming non- processed foods and adapt to practicing clean eating habits. You are what you eat! Why not eat well so you can be well? Your body is the primary vehicle that is going to drive your day. It needs clean fuel daily for a healthy journey. I believe that your body is a temple and should be respected. It's another beautiful way to respect yourself!

I had to take a long look in the mirror and ask myself a serious question, "Am I respecting my temple?" My body is the one place that I have to live in. Therefore, am I giving it the best possible nourishment and treatment to fuel myself for greatness? My answer was NO! I did not have any discipline or a structured diet. I ate uncontrollable amounts of sweets and blamed it on my "sweet tooth." My "good foods" did not outweigh the "bad foods." I thought I had food consumption under control, but I didn't.

I needed to make changes in my diet. One summer while still in college, I was working as a roadside assistance operator, and my body went into complete shock. It felt like I had a mild seizure right in the middle of a phone call. I wasn't able to speak and then the phone shut off. I was trembling and shaking uncontrollably.

What was going on with me? Could it be food poison or some illness?

I hardly ate anything that day. I didn't have an appetite since I was cramping. The only thing I had in my system was two tablets of Midol filled with 750 mg of sodium and 200 mg of heavily salted BBQ chips. This was a recipe for disaster. I had a sodium dosage overload that sent my body into shock! I was only 26 years old when my body felt as if it completely shut down. I fell out of the chair and gasped for air.

I was overreacting a bit, so I got up and went to the nearest fountain to get some water. After that, I regained my full consciousness and could speak again. I tried to make sense of what had happened. It felt as if my nervous system had a pause and couldn't connect to the right receptors for me to speak. It was scary, but I found that It was my diet. Due to salt and sugar being very addictive. Sometimes you don't know when too much is too much, or you don't care until it's too late.

I learned how important it was to take good care of my temple. Gluttony comes in many forms, but it was not going to overtake me! One day, I met a guy in the gym who talked about a nutrition plan to get me in the best shape of my life.

I shrugged it off because I didn't think I needed to lose weight. I was 180 pounds, curvy, and cute. I felt that I needed no improvement. I had to let go of my ego and realistically look at my diet, my body, and most importantly, my results. Even though I initially felt offended that he said I should lose weight, the truth is that I was hiding behind my body's excess fat. I buried my discomfort in Spanx, girdles, and stretchy clothes.

On the first day of my new health plan, I knew nothing about a nutrition plan, clean eating or how it works. However, I did know that if I surrounded myself with positive, energetic, and fit people, my lifestyle would become better. I had to develop the will to be positive about getting in shape, especially when my friends, family, and co-workers didn't believe in me or see my reason for me wanting to get healthy. Be careful of people trying to feed you negativity.

It took courage for me to go to work every day and eat clean. People looked at me in disgust when eating unprocessed foods. Perhaps they felt ashamed or guilty of what they weren't doing for themselves. There were lots of questions like "Why are you doing that?"

To even more inquisitive questions, "Now what are you doing?" I transformed right before their eyes by changing my diet and feeding my body the proper nutrients to fuel my temple for greatness. I learned that to lose weight, working out is only 20% of your progress while 80% is nutrition. I dropped a total of 45 pounds in three months, and I felt the most alive in my life!

Developing proper nutrition educated me on diet,

whole foods, carbohydrates, fitness, and the natural products necessary to support my health goals. I lost the weight very rapidly because I also incorporated meal replacement shakes to keep my calorie intake low and increased my protein intake by eating the right foods. I was able to re-shape my identity and self-love by starting at my core. It had to begin by honoring and taking care of the temple that God created.

Your desire to invest your intellectual capital, internal health & wellness, and self- development should be higher than your desire for material consumption. Material things depreciate. Cars, houses, jewelry, shoes, and clothes come and go. Your faith, education, health, and well-being, although intangible, are everlasting. When you have a firm grasp on your identity, you allow God to do His work to move you towards your purpose.

Society dictates that your material possessions are symbols of your status in life. Some people look at them to judge how far you have "arrived." Automobiles are depreciating assets, but there is a strong affinity to accumulate cars. While working in the automobile industry, I became very knowledgeable about credit, decision-making, purchasing, and buying decisions.

I learned how the automobile industry could take advantage of the disadvantaged and uninformed. Although you may be in desperate need for a vehicle, you must be an educated consumer before making a purchase. A dealer can easily tell you one rate of interest and flip things around to your disadvantage and the next thing you know, you'll pay for a car five times as much that it's worth! Don't throw away thousands of dollars that you don't have. Do your research to make an educated purchase for your best interests.

It would be best if you had a plan and always learn to know yourself better. Strive to understand and discover yourself. It's a journey. Then set an agenda for your goals. Don't allow the media's images to influence your heart and mind. Be sure to do you!

Bettering communities and families also starts with you. Take a long look in the mirror. If you are honest with yourself, you will realize that you are powerful! It's in your DNA to survive and thrive. You don't need anyone to provide what you can provide for yourself. You are capable.

Ask yourself, "Are you living your best life? Do you love yourself fully as a complete individual? Do you create problems or solutions? Are you willing to facilitate an environment that cares about your community? What are you doing to disintegrate the hate and separation that others force may depend upon you? How can you increase love and understanding?"

Your answers are the starting points of getting major work done. Nothing will change until you choose to improve and develop the willpower to love yourself, love others, and do the work. Start living your best life now!

Knowledge, Acknowledgment & Vigilance

As an African-American woman, I had to heal from what I thought beauty represented. I needed to see beauty in myself, not just in some of my features. All of them! I had to stop measuring my beauty on a scale that mainstream dominant societies created. I learned how to set my standards because I discovered that I am the standard. Allowing other people to define your beauty is defying and dishonoring yourself.

Knowing your worth is priceless. It involves understanding your total value. The African Diaspora in America is a complicated, beautiful yet sad, and tumultuous journey. It is my history. My ancestors did not come to America by choice. My very existence on American soil helped build American history to what it is today. Once I was equipped with how to love myself, I became empowered to do more and think better.

Removing the blindfold from your mind reveals the realities of the world. Racial inequalities and social complications still exist no matter how far you are removed from slavery. Staying "woke" is not about being relevant and popular; it's about knowing the truth that is in front of your face. The beauty of acknowledging your past is that you are also honoring your ancestors. Acknowledge their struggles or else you are bound to repeat them. The truth will set you free!

I believe that America should value humanity and celebrate its differences. I see the value in seeing color, but not in classifying it. Seeing color allows you to connect into a rich culture that may not be your own. You can embrace ethnicities and respect differences, not deflect or devalue them.

This begins with tearing down the stereotypes and pre-conceived impressions that you may have. Instead, build up relationships that exceed differences. You cannot help in healing a country until you go forth with an honest conversation about race relations. This cannot continue to be swept under the rug. There's a smell of the horrible stench of racism everywhere.

Now is an excellent time to be open to a conversation with other people who don't look like you. Explore perspectives and see life through another person's lens because if you're not a part of the solution, you can be very much a part of the problem. If you are from an oppressed group, discover practical solutions that can make your community better. One individual can make a difference to do better. Discover your platform and use it to impact change. Silence is acceptance. Don't allow your silence to shield your greatness from emerging.

August Rush

"For I know the plans that I have set before you, plans for you to prosper, not harm you, plans to give you hope and a future."
~ Jeremiah 29:11

In early morning in August 2009, my life hit a turning point. I witnessed a deeper form of love, mercy, and God's unwillingness to let me go. At the time, I kept it inside because of the magnitude that it had on my life. In one hour, I had come to witness the miraculous grace of God before my eyes.

I accepted Christ into my life at age 11. On a breezy fall afternoon, my mother and I were driving on the highway. She asked me, "Shanté have you ever accepted Jesus Christ into your life?"

"I think." I answered.

The car swerved uncontrollably on the highway then onto the shoulder of the road and suddenly came to a halt. She meant business.

As cars started to back up behind us, my mom told me to "Throw your hands up as a form of surrender and repeat after me…Lord, come into my life, lead me every day that I walk this earth."

This was the first time I confessed out loud that God was my Lord. Later, I understood how and why this experience was significant, but I didn't realize it in that very moment. I believed blessings were waiting on me and if I didn't have a relationship with God, I would be lost. When I got older and wiser, I knew the tremendous impact of allowing God to be the leader of my life and take full control of my destiny.

I was living in Phoenix, AZ as a full-fledged young career woman in the banking industry. I was working the night shift clocking out at 2 a.m. It was tiresome, but I managed it well and kept it moving.

A few weeks after my birthday, something significant happened on my way to work. A Ford F-150 pickup truck trampled into the back of my car. My glasses flew off my face, and the In-N-Out burger in my hand slammed into the front windshield. As my body jerked rapidly, my head also hit the window.

What just happened?

I was only a block away from my destination when my car was hit, sliding me into the next lane. I quickly regained control of my car and pulled over to the side of the street. I was impressed with how rapid my reflexes were. Then I fell into complete shock from what just happened. Because of the trauma, I didn't experience any pain. However, when I tried to get out of the car, my whole body became instantly stiff. Since I was hurt, I sat in my car and called the police.

Still in shock, I pushed my way straight to the hospital. A few x-rays were taken, and I was released to go home. I contemplated taking the rest of the week off work because my body was unstable and ached. I didn't want to let my team down, so I pulled it together and went to work.

I prayed that the next day would be better. I picked up the pieces and got everything back on track. I rented a car that I would later find out had a gas gage problem. After I got off work before the crack of dawn, the rental vehicle stopped in the middle of the highway. It occurred adjacent to a desert road next to a cactus patch and tumbleweeds. I calmly, but quickly, maneuvered pulling off the road into a safe location to call for help. The problem was that my phone was dead! There I waited as multiple cars filled with men approached me. I declined their assistance because I did not feel safe. A few minutes later, a young lady who looked around my age pulled up and asked if I needed help.

My intuition gave me a better feeling about her. She took me up the roadway to get gas and drove me back to the rental car. Suddenly, I discovered that the car keys were locked inside! I couldn't believe all of my misfortune, but I moved on and put gas in the car. Upon doing so, I felt a bit of condensation above my head. A tiny storm cloud formed above me and stretched across the highway. Hurriedly, I jumped back into the lady's car. I decided it was best for me to get back home and then come back for the rental car later on with my roommate.

When we arrived at my apartment community, the parking gate wouldn't open because my gate code didn't work. How ironic! I thanked the woman who helped me and walked the remainder of the way to my apartment. It was about 4:30 in the morning and random thoughts were rushing in my head. A large part of me wanted to break down, fold up, and cry. As the tears welled up in my eyes, my faith wouldn't let me give up. What was I to make of these epic series of unfortunate events? Was this the way things were going to be from here on out?

When I entered my apartment, my roommate looked at me and noticed the distress upon my face. She asked, "Are you okay?" I couldn't speak. I shook my head in disbelief. I was filled with grief and despair. I went to my room and sat on my bed. My roommate came in and asked, "Do I need to call your mother?" I shook my head again. Then I finally gathered the strength to ask her, "Can you take me to my car?" She agreed, and we left to retrieve the rental car from the highway exit.

When I finally reached the vehicle, highway patrol pulled up behind it to keep from blocking traffic. The car still wouldn't start so I called AAA then sat on the passenger's side of my roommate's car. I remember looking up towards the sky. By now, I had stopped crying, but I wasn't able to talk about what just happened. I was still in pain from my car accident.

My roommate sensed I had a hard time, so she waited with me in silence. I knew that if I talked, my tears would fall endlessly. Then I heard the voice of

God asking, "Do you trust me?" I answered in my heart and spirit, "Yes." There was nothing more to worry about.

Immediately, I had reassurance in knowing that tests, trials, and setbacks are a part of life. God had equipped me with everything I need to survive and enabled me to bear up under my burdens by His grace. I was reminded that God handpicked my circumstances to accomplish a specific purpose.

No matter how sketchy, illogical, or misfortunate times may seem, I trust that I am covered because God's love seeks nothing for itself but gives generously out of its abundance. Believing in God when you don't have the answer is the perfect roadmap and lifeline to call on. This is how I've witnessed riding out the storms in life. You should be still enough to hear the voice of God and to be receptive to it.

So often, you want immediate answers to your problems when you pray. You build microwave prayer requests demanding a thirty-second delivery. God may have another plan. He offers a different method of delivery for you to have a clearer vision on the other side of your journey.

Sometimes God will take you through a particular situation to prepare you for your next destination. I believe that my circumstances are also my life's blessings even though I wished they could have unfolded differently. Because I am a child of God, I know that I am covered.

Living in the desert was one of my loneliest times, but I was never left alone. God was with me the entire time. These events confirmed that my time in the desert was coming to an end. A new journey was awaiting elsewhere.

I've been blessed to experience and learn many lessons. I am not ashamed of any of them. These life lessons have brought me to a fulfillment that I never thought I would ever experience. I'm a beautiful reflection of adversity, persistence, grace, wisdom, and valor all rolled up into one. My footsteps walk this path because I know that I am destined for greatness. My voice triumphs into victories because my failures are catalysts for change and progress.

Gratitude, Grace & Gravity (Humbleness)

The chaotic, crazy, and unstable times are vital. They challenge you to rise to a high level of consciousness and help you to become a problem-solver. You are more alert and aware of the situations around you. Often when things go wrong, you may reach for religion. This allows your faith to become stronger by talking to God a lot more. What would happen if you did this every day? What if you let God speak to you or you spent more time with Him? Imagine being receptive to the voice of God through your everyday experiences. I connect to the creator in my own way. I believe you can too. Each of my experiences has humbled me. As a child of God, I dwell in His presence and wait for His direction. This gives me such inner-peace.

All the things that I endured brought me to a place of humility that I never experienced before. This type of humility was like gravity, and it brought me to my knees. This season in my life assured me that no matter what my job title is or bank account looks like, God is in control. He truly showed me grace and mercy. My faith was tested, and God came and rescued me in the midnight hour. If I did not survive that situation, I might have had to learn about His presence in another way. If you've experienced the love of God and His grace, it is indeed a blessing. If you are wondering if God loves you and if He protects you, seek Him first. There is no greater love than the love of God.

When things are chaotic, be still and let God work. You may feel tired, upset, unstable, borderline crazy or even frustrated. That's okay. Having the courage to be still in a difficult situation is key to overcoming your storm. I could have broken down, got angry or panicked on the highway when things started to get bad. That would have only escalated my frustrations and the problem. You won't have good judgment when you act on emotion. You make irrational decisions that have no benefit to you in the end. Allow yourself to be still and let God work on your behalf.

Find the lessons in your storm. Ride it out! You don't want the same storms to reoccur in your life. It is wise to learn those lessons now. What do you want your life to be filled with? Joy and satisfaction? Or anger and destruction? Be open to learning from your mistakes and develop your patterns to take you down a path towards greatness. It's critical to living the abundant life God has designed for you.

Phoenix Rise

"Think like a queen. A queen is not afraid to fail.
Failure is another steppingstone to greatness."
~ Oprah Winfrey

Will the lightest skin win the competition? "No!"
"Will the prettiest hair win the competition? "No!"
"Will the lightest eyes win the competition? No!
"What wins competitions?
"Consistency!" I exalted to the top of my lungs.

I was in full force boot camp competing to win the title
for Miss Black Arizona USA. I made it as a state finalist, and
I knew I could win. The former Miss Black Arizona USA
was one of my coaches. She also inspired me to believe that
I could win. My coach was a pivotal part of my growth during my preparation. This period of my life went far beyond
a pageant.

The word Phoenix has been associated with the sun,
obtaining new life by arising from the ashes of its predeces-
sor. The bird-like symbol of the Phoenix was used as a symbol in early Christianity. Phoenix is a major metropolitan
city of the United States, but for me, it's a symbolic representation of the awakening of a destiny.

While shopping in Target, my phone buzzed in my pocket. "Is this Miss Shaun-tay Berry?" It was the powerful voice of a former Miss Black Arizona USA. She enunciated my name in her no-nonsense, Chicago accent. "We need you in the pageant this year. You are competing again right?"

I didn't know that she remembered my name let alone had my phone number. I heard her speak before at a pageant meeting. Her confidence and poise enamored me. Her voice was powerful, and her beauty was impeccable. She was about business. I was captivated as soon as I heard her voice. She also coached other girls and mentored them in the pageant system. Each one soared to the top of the charts and won or as she would say, "take the pageant."

This woman instilled in me, a great deal of confidence, charisma, and most importantly, consistency. The prettiest face does not win the pageant, the lightest skin does not win the pageant, and the longest hair does not win the pageant. What does? Consistency wins the pageant! She did more than prepare me for the pageant; she taught me how to be unapologetically brilliant. If I doubted myself for one second, I had given the competition away. I had to make up my mind first that it was my time to win. She eloquently taught me that I always had to hold my head high or the crown would fall. I had to be my authentic self and leave a lasting and memorable impression on the judges and crowd. What makes you stand out and what will you be remembered for?

My goal was to move the judges in a way where they fell

completely in love with me, and they wouldn't see anybody else fit for the title, but me. I became active in the Miss Black Arizona scholarship pageant for social reasons, but God had so much more for me! This experience enriched my life, and I never looked at pageants the same. It became my new sport. I trained, I practiced, I perfected my skills, and I got out and showed the world what I was made of. The only difference in this sport was that I went straight to the finals. There weren't any practice rounds or semifinals. I thought I had everything it took to win and the truth is...I did. However, I had to peel a couple of layers of my shell to discover it. I learned never to be afraid to receive coaching and feedback. It's for your own good. Don't run away from criticism, listen. It helps develop you!

For the next four months, I trained for the pageant. It was intense emotionally, mentally, and physically. Physical training was the first thing on the agenda that I perfected. I knew that I couldn't just show up pretty. I had to put in the work and be ready to compete. I spent 1-2 hours a day standing in heels with feet positioned 2 and 10 o'clock. I would recite my introduction to myself in the car over and over and practice my monologue all night until I heard birds chirping the next morning.

I would visualize myself competing up until the day it happened. For the pageant's creative category, I would perform my first theatrical poem. I was far from nervous because I perfected my craft performing at many open-mics for spoken word. I was excited, ready, and I couldn't wait! When the big day came, I left a piece of my soul on the stage. The audience in the 500-seat theater heard every word of my poem. I invited them into my personal narrative of how I had to find a way back to school after Hurricane Katrina. My poem, "No Answer" had a fast-paced rhythm that took you through my horrific journey of riding it out in the storm to finally graduating on stage.

Performing was my passion that I successfully turned into a sport. In place of a swimsuit competition, the pageant had a personal fitness competition. This allowed me as a young lady to reveal my personality through sports and recreation. I could choose anything from track and field to motorcycle racing. Little did I know that all my dreaming and preparation led me to become Miss Black Arizona USA.

This experience was so valuable to me that whatever the outcome, I walked away a better, well- rounded person. The pageant challenged me in ALL areas. The first time I competed, I won 2nd runner-up. The following year, I competed again and won 1st runner- up. As favor would have it, the next year I was appointed to hold the title as Miss Black Arizona USA 2011. I was excited to have the title and platform, but it was short-lived. It wasn't too long before I moved out of the state of Arizona. Sometimes victories are bittersweet, and the journey is more rewarding than having the crown.

My dreams wake me up in the middle of the night. They ask me, "Who will give me feet to walk? Who will give me a mouth to speak? Who will give me wings to fly and be free?"

My most cherished moments were when I dared to look my fears in the eye without blinking. I took on tasks head-on, not knowing what I would have to endure or what the outcome could be. The tasks weren't easy, but I kept riding it out.

I was quiet and reserved growing up. Once I began to blossom, I started to know who I was. I learned to develop my voice, but I was very uncomfortable expressing it. Could it have been fear? Rejection? Being judged? I'm not sure what made me hold back as a child. However, the root of my reserved nature was identified when I discovered a true platform to stand on. My whole perspective changed the fall semester of my senior year of high school. My voice would be defined.

At age seventeen, I stepped up to the podium with boldness in my spirit and a declaration in my heart. I sought after the highest office in my high school, Senior Class President. This season will forever represent new beginnings for me. I was filled with the expectancy of reaching new educational heights and growing into the young woman that I wanted to be. The wind was filled with anticipation. I knew that no matter what the results were, I had already achieved great things by overcoming my fear and letting my voice be heard.

The night before my speech, I walked into my dad's room and asked, "Dad, do you want to hear my speech?"

I proudly read my mono-toned, one-minute speech to him. He was unmoved.

He looked me in the face and asked, "Do you want to win the vote or just give a speech?"

I shouted, "I want to win, Dad!"

In a severe and determined tone, he said, "Well let's give

a winning speech then."

For the next hour and a half, I rehearsed my speech as if I was preparing to give it at the White House.

I belted out tones and word rhythms in ways that I had never heard them before. I was amazed at myself and the voice inside of me. That evening, my dad coached me and helped me discover my own voice. I've often wondered if it wasn't for my dad coaching me, would I have ever found it? How beautiful the experience is for a young girl to discover the power of her voice. It took me about 60 minutes to learn how to be a compelling speaker.

The next day, I stepped up to the podium at school and flawlessly delivered my candidacy speech as rehearsed. I gave it the same power and delivery from practicing it the night before. I ended my speech with a timeless saying, "Sometimes the best man for the job is a woman!" Then I dropped the mic, and the audience cheered in victory.

My class loved the speech, but I, unfortunately, lost the vote to a boy! I noticed that some of the boys had a peculiar look on their faces. Some may have taken offense to the fact that I chose to end my speech in a "girls rock" statement. Nevertheless, I went home happy as I won the nomination for Class Vice-President. The boy who won Senior Class President did a great job. Together, we led our class as I offered support to him along the way.

I thought about the preparation and what if I had not stepped up. I had gained much more confidence by conquering my fear of public speaking. I realized when I stepped up to the mic that my tone and confidence changed.

I stretched entirely out of my shell.

That is why it is crucial for you to find your own voice. There is strength in your voice. There is no greater force than a man or woman determined to rise. When you discover that your power determines your possibilities, your mindset will change, and your attitude will change as well. The world will open to you!

If you never had a mother or father figure in your life to guide and help you find your power, you should connect with someone whom you feel is a powerful and influential role model. Ask that person to be your mentor or advisor. Someone whom you can soak up information from, gain wisdom, knowledge, and find strength from their testimonies and experiences.

From that point on, I had the ambition to succeed. I did my best in every area. The sky was the limit. I knew that I would have to work for whatever I wanted in life. I also knew that I had God on my side to help me get there.

During my senior year of high school, I sought every academic and extracurricular scholarship I possibly could. I wanted to position myself as a strong candidate by interviewing, writing essays, and sending letters. Searching for scholarships became an extracurricular activity. It didn't matter if I didn't hear back from some of the organizations. What mattered was that I wrote to them for opportunities. I had two scholarship resource books and one main website called Fastweb. I wrote every organization a letter for an application. I wanted to let them know that I needed an opportunity to succeed academically and that not going to college wasn't an option.

Endless opportunities started to unfold as I wrote letters to businesses and applied for different scholarships. My favorite part of the day was coming home from school and opening my mail. My dad would put the letters on top of the television. Every day I had a different response awaiting me and each one was a gift.

I had a competitive grade point average, and my extracurricular activities were extensive. However, I never anticipated receiving all the financial support and responses that I did. I connected with my guidance counselor, and I was always in her office seeking further opportunities. By the time high school graduation came, I had accumulated a four-year annual total of $50,000 in scholarships alone. I was accepted to my top five universities and discovered what favor was early in life. I felt it and knew that every letter and every penny came from the grace of God. I never took any of my opportunities for granted. I maintained the right mindset and knew that opportunities existed. I discovered the beautiful formula that A's and B's = G's. G's = Grand.

After my high school triumphs, I was unstoppable. I felt a power that every young person should feel. Opportunities opened in every direction, and I knew my future success didn't have any boundaries. I took the limits off my mind and truly started to gear up to aim even higher.

As an avid reader and writer, I saw myself naturally develop into a poet. I wrote lyrics and poems with my child-hood friends, and I titled my first poetry book, Susie's Kitchen.

Before performing, I would ask people, "Are you ready to eat in Suzie's kitchen?"

My family would yell, "Yeah!"

I knew it wouldn't be the last time I performed. I wrote rhymes, and I loved the exciting wordplay that I could weave together to make the right sounds and definition. My poetic writing was like scrabble gone wild, yet very thera-peutic and humbling. The words came from the place where my deepest emotions resided. It wasn't until several years later, I would be comfortable with getting in front of a room full of strangers and pouring my heart out on the stage.

These experiences brought confidence, posture, charac-ter, extreme self-expression, and proper enunciation. I was better prepared to speak in front of crowds and felt com-fortable at the same time. Once the microphone was in my hand, I owned that moment. Every experience was an op-portunity for me to capture the attention of strangers mak-ing memorable moments.

For the next few years, I performed more and more. It was always a chance for me to get on stage and reach various people. Throughout my travels between school and work, I performed. I shared my spoken word in multiple cities such as New Orleans, New York, Los Angeles Atlanta, Houston, Chicago, Phoenix, and Memphis. I was gracious to touch different cultures and regions of people with my creative work. I never knew whose ears my words would fall upon with inspiration to change their life. My message was always of hope and developing the will to keep going!

The semester after Hurricane Katrina, I applied for an internship in New York. I needed to do something progressive to uplift my spirit. I took a chance. I didn't have any prior experience in the editorial field, but I put my heart into my application – everything from art, poetry, and essays. New York took me entirely by surprise. During the spring of my junior year of college, I received a phone call of interest while taking a study break.

The voice on the other side of the phone asked, "Hello. Is this Shanté, Shanté Berry?"

"This is she." I answered.

It was a lady named Marisol from Essence Magazine. "We want you to join our staff this summer!"

I was in complete euphoria. I busted out screaming on the fourth floor of my school library. My trip to New York marked a new beginning of another journey. A journey of more profound self-discovery, independence, and greater definition to my life. As I began my transition to New York, I realized that it would not be an easy one. I had to stabilize housing, but I didn't have the necessary funds. I decided to have a fundraiser so I could get up and go to New York.

I took my ideas to Natural Bridge and Fair in my hometown of Saint Louis. I did a quick fundraiser for washing cars. My dad brought the speakers out, my momma made the signs, and my friends and family came out on a hot Saturday to lend a hand to wash and support. I raised nearly four hundred dollars! This helped me immensely with my transition expenses. It didn't take care of all my expenses, but it was four hundred more dollars than I started with.

At twenty-one years old, I was on the plane headed to New York. I had a lot to see and do, a lot to seek out, thousands of people to meet, and countless places to go. Who would have thought that an inner-city black girl would pave her pathway to New York to work for America's number-one magazine for African American women? I couldn't believe my single application made an impact and stood out from the other applicants.

Each day in New York was an absolute learning experience. Over the first two weeks at Essence, I gained an abundance of opportunities, work, and a wealth of knowledge. From the first day meeting with my co-worker and Marissa, there was a special kind of connection. Our manager, Cherie told me that the magazine is less like a business and more like a family. The interns in my group and I worked hard as a team, and we kept each other motivated. I felt that my experience at Essence would be truly significant in the company. I had a bigger purpose than being a summer intern. A mission that was larger than me. I could make a difference. I thanked God for surrounding me with the right people and moving me in the right direction.

My co-worker and I had to realize that we were not each other's competition, but each other's assets. We were young, gifted women-of-color with different contributions to bring to the table. As interns, we were not exclusive to what we did, what we learned, to whom we'd meet, and what we set out to do. I was encouraged to seek opportunities everywhere.

My co-worker and I could do anything we wanted, but together we could do more! The competition was all around us. Many times, you worry about staying "on top." I didn't feel like that was necessary for me. I believe that everyone contributes to a common goal. I thanked God for helping me take a step closer to my dreams.

While at a particular work event, my contact lenses started getting cloudy and I couldn't see! Then my eyes burned as something had highly irritated them. I rushed to the bathroom and noticed three women. They were all different ages standing at the faucet talking. At first, I didn't speak, and I was in pain from my eyes itching. Then they saw me struggling to rinse my eyes in the sink. The ladies stopped checking their makeup and asked if I was ok. The ladies even had eye solution and napkins to help nurse me back to good health. Complete strangers!

We instantly became sisters. They could have walked out and said, "Sucks for her." Thank God they didn't. I only wished that I saw more of this kindness — women who help each other, not hurt each other. Whether you are friends or an associate, the negativity, cattiness, jealousy or hate should be far removed when connecting with one another. When I walked out of the ladies' room, I felt great! I met three strangers who cared about my well-being, and I felt instantly better.

Surprisingly, I saw those three ladies the next day. We were at an upscale event. I was checking tickets at the door when we recognized each other. We hugged right there! I didn't even know their names, but I knew the kindness of their hearts. That interaction meant everything to me. It sparked joy! I thought about it over the next few days. What if we experienced kindness every day? Imagine if strangers spoke, listened, and cared about you expecting nothing in return? It all starts with you.

My time in New York was so short, so I made every day very impactful. I woke up one morning with an ambition to exercise, so I went running. My roommate joined me. We ran half of the Brooklyn Bridge and back. My roommate, Denise was from Brooklyn, and we clicked on the spot from day one. She was into fitness, shopping, cooking, and natural hair. Denise was such a huge blessing because she helped me settle in the Big Apple. She taught me on safety, so I could protect myself when traveling to work in Manhattan. I would jog across the Brooklyn Bridge most mornings, and it set the tone for my whole day. My goal was to beat the light signal on my final round. I did just that. Again, I was unstoppable. I felt that I could do the impossible and see the imaginable if I put my mind to it. That's precisely what I did.

I absorbed as much as I could in the editorial and media industry. Usually, this takes years to attain. The publishing industry fluctuates with job positions coming and going so I had to keep relevant, marketable, and competitive. However, I gained much more than knowledge about the publishing world. This internship gave me bold confidence and clear direction. I learned to conquer my career goals. I will never forget my last day at Essence. In one word, Amazing!

I was very thankful for that summer. It confirmed that I was right where I needed to be. God had turned my life around. In less than one year after riding it out with Hurricane Katrina, I was interning for the summer at Essence. God was good to me, and my hard work paid off when I least expected it.

My summer internship went fast! It lasted only eight weeks, but I knew it had to end. It was a once-in-a-lifetime opportunity, from networking, developing professionally, establishing friendships, and creating business relationships. It allowed me to shine! I gave my talents to Essence, but I also shared my testimony too. I was rejuvenated and equipped for a better future. I never felt more powerful! My time in New York had been enriching. God gave me the chance to see opportunities, take them, travel, and meet new people. You never know what you can do until you give it all you got and step out on faith.

Character, Competition & Consistency

Your character can take you far beyond where money ever can. Consistency is the vehicle that will get you there. The only competition that you have is yourself. There is no one else in the world like you! No one has the same DNA as you. Even identical twins have significant differences in their personality and character. It's what helps you tell them apart. It's completely fine to embrace your uniqueness. This is why it's vital to work daily on developing your character by continually feeding your mind with reinforcing positive affirmations. For as a man thinketh in his heart so is he.viii

If you listen to negative thoughts, negativity can spiral into your actions. When you feed your spirit with positivity, encouragement, and wisdom, you have no choice but to grow and be uplifted. You will at some point run low on motivational fuel. Just like your body needs fuel to go on so does your mind and spirit. Find a motivational speaker that you like and devote fifteen minutes daily to listen to their messages. It would be best if you were committed and consistent with giving yourself the right fuel.

Realize that your biggest competitor is in the mirror. You are the first person to hear your thoughts. Words cut like knives. You don't have to believe what everyone tells you about yourself, especially if it does not agree with your spirit. If you have people around you who don't speak to your inner greatness, then you are going to live with their bitterness. Don't let them rob you of your inner-strength and light. Don't allow Satan to rent-free space in your head or heart. Give him an immediate eviction notice.

Make time for hobbies and surround yourself with positive, motivated people. Healthy hobbies such as painting, bike riding or building something. Do something that contributes and gives back to you! Find hobbies that cause you to grow and mature. Destructive hobbies will distract you from your purpose. The temporary high that you get from anything destructive will eventually bring you to an all-time low. Invest your time wisely in activities that expand your mind and mature you as a person.

A goal without consistency is a wish. Thoughts become things when we are consistent and working towards them.

Make it happen! What goals are you not being compatible with that you have been trying to conquer for years? When you silence your fears, it is incredible what you can accomplish with focus. You must be willing to nurture, develop, and execute your dreams into reality. Greatness is the result of escaping excuses, executing faith, and delivering hard work.

Get Out

"I'm reclaiming my time!"
~Maxine Waters

My eyes were wide open, but I could not move my legs, hands or feet. All I could do is accept the fact that I'm alive and breathing. This was not a dream. I felt paralyzed with no control of my body. Mentally I knew I was strong, so why can't I get up? Why can't I rise out of this? I tried to talk, but I could barely mumble. As I laid in bed, no one was going to get me out of this, but me. I calmed myself down from the panic attack. I closed my eyes to return to a light sleep in the hope that I would wake up fully alert.

A half an hour later, I woke up alert and thankful that my body woke up with me. It was the scariest thing! I researched what I experienced and found out I had gone through a series of rapid eye movements in the sleep cycle. This is where the brain is still in REM (rapid eye movement). It's the cycle that you have before you wake up and the body has not gotten the signal to wake up yet.

The condition is called sleep paralysis. Here, the body remains paralyzed in REM atonia while the brain awakens and the eyes start to open. Sleep paralysis can occur during one of two transitions in the sleep cycle. The body must go into REM sleep, and it must come out of it. Sleep paralysis occurs when the body has trouble making these transitions. This can happen to anyone that is under a lot of stress.

This wasn't the first time I had experienced sleep paralysis, but I was eager to know what was causing it. I went to the doctor and had tests run. The findings reported that I was stressed and needed adequate rest. This proved to be true as I reflected on my lifestyle. I had recently moved to a new city, started a new job, and had a new apartment. Much adaptation and transitions were going on, and I was handling it the best way I could. My shift to a new city was affecting my transition to sleep.

It made sense to me. I decided at that point to focus on self-care and getting better rest. Relaxing, taking a warm bath before bed, soothing music, or whatever it took to relax before I transitioned to sleep completely. I could no longer crash on the couch after dinner in front of the TV and expect to have a restful night's sleep. It made a world of difference! The sleep paralysis stopped when I started to master my self-care process. I thought about this stagnation in sleep cycles and transitions. I compared it to the periods of shifts and recession that I had previously experienced in my life and what I did to get out.

In the winter of 2017, the world was introduced to the movie Get Out, a sci-fi psychological thriller. It took the viewer on an experience to a sunken place in which the main character, Chris, goes into a deeper state of conscious and cannot move. He is stuck and cannot go anywhere while under hypnosis.

How many of us feel this way from day-to-day? Many times, you are stuck! You cannot get that new job, the new car, the new house or even the healthy stable relationship that you seek. You try to do different things but get the same results. Or worse, you do the same things and expect different results. You feel as though the conditions and systems that you have been placed in or born in have paralyzed you. No matter how hard it gets, you have to keep going toward your goal. Ride it out!

There were several times when I felt completely paralyzed and stuck in a job, a city or a relationship when I knew I could do much better. Because of challenging life circumstances, you stay where you are. You do this because you are comfortable, and you don't see any other options. You remain complacent. It seems easier to be in a comfortable hell when you are afraid of uncomfortable heaven. Since you are afraid of something new or different, you are paralyzed from living up to your full potential.

This has happened to me, and many times, I've felt trapped and unhappy. I let immaturity and ego get the best of me. When I left Phoenix, AZ, I also left a wonderful job where I was thriving professionally. My personal life was another story. I was unhappy, depressed, unfulfilled, and extremely lonely so I left everything and went back home to live with my family. Ego and bad advice told me, "You're college educated, independent, and a successful woman. You can easily build this again if you walk away." Instead of trusting God's plan and weathering through that rough time, I wanted to get out of my state of unhappiness.

Sometimes getting out by jumping out is not always the best thing to do. Timing is everything. If it is your season to be in a situation where God is building something better in you, it is wise to stay in the storm and bloom where you are planted. I learned the hard way. I was welcomed home to the coldest winter ever and unemployment. It took me losing something valuable to appreciate what I had.

If you have to force anything, it probably isn't a good fit. I try not to have regrets in life, but there are times when I could have made better-informed decisions. Every failure is a lesson. I'm still living, breathing, and progressing. You cannot let failures restrict you from growing, but uplift you towards greater heights. Make sure that those mistakes are not repeated. Don't go through life floating from one destination to the next, but rather be intentional towards a higher purpose.

Sometimes this feeling of paralysis is how being black in America can feel like to me. I can't fully express myself or my culture because I may lose my job, status, money or something else precious to me. I feel completely paralyzed. My hair is too curly and coiled. My name is too ethnic or cultured. The way I enunciate my words gives off too much of an accent or urban vernacular.

Have you ever felt paralyzed in life? Do you want to express an emotion, but don't because it could be interpreted as rage? The problem is that I'm not angry, I only want to be able to live my truth and be. This leads to feelings of being controlled. Have you ever experienced being managed by someone who doesn't have your best interests at heart? Were you ever worried that if you broke free from the bondage holding you back, it might be labeled as something else? Being paralyzed often occurs from unjust wrongs, yet you can't express it without suffering consequences.

You want the job, you are qualified for the job, but you alter your name to sound less ethnic for fear of being discriminated because of your race. What happens next when you're suddenly under or overqualified for the position? They found a "better fit." Deep down you knew you had all the qualifications and skills.

When you are operating in your full authentic self, and you fit the qualifications, but it doesn't give you the results you want, what do you do? Be creative and find a solution! If the job that you desired doesn't want to hire you, hire yourself. Get out of the places where you are not growing and advancing as you should be. However, know your season to plan, prepare, and execute the move. Get out of toxic dead-end relationships or situations that do not propel you towards your purpose. Life is too precious to be in a position where you are not valued and celebrated. Getting out doesn't always mean jumping out of the window (unless your life is threatened, then, by all means, get out!). Instead, it's finding a ladder to climb and get to the next window. You are worthy and deserve a chance to build a beautiful life. Make smart choices today that push you towards that happy place of tomorrow.

I once had a job where I felt like a robot. I would recite the same script every day for eight hours. I had the same time for lunch and breaks every day. It was if my brain would overheat and explode if I read the script one more time. I knew that I wasn't living up to my full potential and my gifts and abilities were not used effectively. I got out!

I consciously developed a plan to get out of the job that paralyzed me. If you feel stuck in something and don't know how to get out, planning is the best preparation for success. If you keep hitting a brick wall with your planning, rest, reevaluate, and reset your mind. Come back with a better plan to execute. Make a goal every day and make progress. If you are trying to find another job, apply to at least 20 job posts a day to maximize your opportunities. Today is a new day to get right back up and work on being great!

Transition, Travel & Taking Back Your Identity

The shifts that you go through in life can help you advance if you are not afraid to let them. You can escape your fear of change by embracing change. It's the doorway to greatness. Traveling helps expand your horizons and gives you a new perspective. It also gives you an avenue to meet new people.

When I am traveling, I feel limitless, eager, ready to learn, and grow. Learning about new cultures, languages, foods, and customs shapes your view of the world and makes you more diverse. Diversity means being different, but it should not be distant or disrespectful. These types of experiences are priceless. When you expand your horizons, the world becomes so much bigger than your block. It's important to renew, refresh, and immerse yourself in new environments.

You may find yourself in situations where someone wants you to be something that you are not. Recognize when that is not healthy and stand up for who you are and what you represent. Learn to adapt to the diversity of others, but also be ok with receiving criticism. There is a difference between constructive criticism and when someone is criticizing to tear you down and break your spirit. Develop the discernment to know the difference and recognize it when you interact with people. I've learned that constructive criticism uplifts. If you learn the difference, then you can be open to facilitate more opportunities for maturity and growth.

Fear is a liar! When you stay stagnant in the place that isn't a progressive for you, fear will cause you to do a disservice to yourself. You may be comfortable but being uncomfortable inspires growth that you need to reach your full potential. Taking back your identity requires courage and faith to come against the factors in society that may try to shield your identity. Your mission should be centered on living your best life as your true authentic self.

As the author, Marianne Williamson says, "It is our light, not our darkness that most frightens us. Who am I to be brilliant, gorgeous, talented, and fabulous?' Who are you not to be? Your playing small does not serve the world. We were born to make manifest the glory of God that is within us. It's not just in some of us; it's in everyone." Get out of your relationship with complacency and step into your greatness!

Guns and Roses

"Love makes your soul crawl out from its hiding place"
~Zora Neale Hurston

He killed her." My cousin cried through the phone. "Who did what?" I responded.

During my time living in Los Angeles, I received a strange phone call at work. My cousin was on the other end of the receiver sobbing horrifically. I knew that something was instantly not right. I rose from my seat in a panic to know what was going on. I had an idea of who she was talking about, but my heart sank further into my chest at that thought.

A part of me didn't want to know. I mentioned a few names, but after saying the first few letters of Lydia's name, I knew it was her. Lydia was my cousin's close friend. She also became a close friend to me. Her husband had killed her. He shot her in broad daylight at an amusement park back at home in St. Louis, MO. They were in the process of divorcing, but still living under the same roof. They had three small children so they were trying their best to make a difficult marriage situation work until the divorce was final.

No one expected it to go to this extreme. Lydia had such a radiant, jovial, and creative spirit as well as an appreciation for life and culture. I learned a lot from each conversation I had with her. What I didn't know was that Lydia's relationship with her husband was verbally abusive, which quickly and often escalated to physical abuse. I'm guessing she kept the severity of the situation to herself to avoid alarming to her family and friends.

Losing Lydia hit me extremely hard. I felt for her children and family members because they wouldn't ever see her again. The last time I spoke with Lydia, I sensed that there was fear in her heart, but I never imagined this outcome. A lot of relationships struggle with control and communication issues. Not having control can be a person's worst fear.

As for Lydia, her estranged husband had lost total control. He took her life and his too. Over the next few weeks, Lydia appeared in my dreams. She expressed how her life was in danger. Somehow, she knew it before she was murdered. It was devastating to me. Every time I woke up from these nightmares, I couldn't believe how Lydia and I were laughing on the phone one minute, and now she was gone the next.

I believe God gives you warning signs in relationships. It's up to you to choose to acknowledge those signs or ignore them. That's the moment when everything stops, and you make a decision that can save your life. I'm grateful that I took my time in developing friendships, especially with men who showed interest in me. I never wanted to be involved in a toxic relationship and paid attention to any events that could have lead up to that.

Relationships usually don't start toxic. Typically, the 'toxic' part develops over time. Toxic relationships take more out of you than it gives back. They may temporarily feel great at times, only to come crashing down moments later because of a critical imbalance. Being unequally yoked is a painful reality, but it's important to recognize for the health and growth of a relationship.

I learned many lessons about relationships in the years to follow. You do not have to accept what you attract. I believe that a lot of people and things can be drawn to you, but it is what you allow to persist that is important. My gut can tell me more than time does. My inner voice tells me you knew this would be the outcome.

If you accept less than what you know you deserve, find the reason why. Evaluate your self-esteem and redefine what you will and won't tolerate to honor yourself. Set firm boundaries and enforce them. Think and speak positively to feel better about yourself and to create a healthy reality. Your frequency of thought gives rise to certain emotions that then give rise to your actions. Your thoughts control your decisions and actions. Think good thoughts and watch how situations turn out.

Love is about finding someone you never thought you'd meet. It welcomes positive energy and helps to take your life in a new direction. I once had a stronger connection with someone that I only held hands with during a date versus a person who I kissed and cuddled within a relationship.

The right chemistry, spirituality, and mental connection

can surpass any amount of physical contact. A physical relationship is pointless without being equally 'yoked.' Giving your body to a person is powerful enough in itself, too powerful to be meaningless.

I saved myself from a boatload of heartaches by committing myself to abstinence starting in my youth. It was a very positive enforcement in my life. I was aware that the bible says to present your body as a living sacrifice. I understood my body is not even my own do what I pleased with it. Instead is it a temple where my soul and spirit dwell. Why allow everyone and anyone into your temple. It is a sacred place. To abstain from the desires of the flesh, that will war against your soul.

I recognized that there is no peace outside of the will of God. I desire to have God's best and abstinence made life less complicated and helped me focus on more important things. I looked at premarital sex as the only thing that would keep me from my life goals such as finishing my education, traveling and establishing myself. Especially if I had the enormous responsibility of having to raise a child on my own. A lot of women have had children early and unmarried, but I'm sure they could attest that life was harder. My mother made it her business to inform me about abstinence early. I made up my mind and knew right away that I was not going to get involved in sexual relations in my youth and beyond. I bypassed a lot of confusion and complications by remaining abstinent.

Many young men and women are still trying to find themselves in their early 20s. I believe the best time to date is when you are more mature and somewhat older and established. People will drift away and then reappear, but it's critical to be a complete person.

The key that I've learned is that everybody you date doesn't deserve your heart. Guarding your heart can be the smartest and healthiest thing you can do for yourself when you're dating. You should safeguard your heart from lonely strangers, dead situations that try to come back to resurface, and particularly people who have not proven themselves deserving of your time and attention. Everyone will not have the same agenda as you. Protect your heart, mind, and emotions like you would a rare diamond rather than leaving it exposed like a stray rock.

The first time I fell in love was when my eyes gazed across the table at Morris. *At this time I knew nothing about protecting my heart.* His eyes pierced into my soul. He tried to decipher what was on my mind, but I failed to express to him what I felt. I thought Morris couldn't handle the fact that I saw him as a beautiful creation of God. A young king who was waiting to make his mark on the world. Morris was close to everything I wanted in a man. I finally felt like this man was worth my time and energy. Our phone conversations were endless. I knew Morris from my past. We had history attending the same school. He was an old classmate. I remember him being very handsome. I reconnected with Morris on social media. I was optimistic about dating him, but I knew I would have to be very cautious about the process. People do a lot of pretending online and a lot of time had passed since I last saw Morris.

Today the world is cyber-connected; everything is done online. School, work, and friendships are common on the internet. Therefore, it wasn't odd to reconnect with Morris this way. I am a believer that if you open yourself to whatever you're seeking, you will find it or better yet it will find you!

Certain people are a joy to be around, and my father is one of them. Morris was much like my father, very confident and well-spoken. Wise beyond his years and sensitive to my thoughts. He was a true gentleman and valued my opinion. With each conversation, we fed each other words and shared our dreams. We never ran out things to discuss. Our friendship was genuine.

The courtship began late in the winter, a little bit after the New Year. The year was fresh and so was our energy. We talked on the phone extensively. He enjoyed my spunk and personality, and I enjoyed his mystery and curiosity. His calm energy enlightened me along with his rational expressions and knowledge about a variety of topics. I hadn't been intrigued in a while. He was well- traveled and well-versed, I knew we had chemistry from our very first conversation.

Morris made claims that I took him by storm, captured his attention, and mesmerized him on purpose. All I did was be myself. I grew more and more attracted to him week after week. Even if I was physically attracted to someone, it had little to do with me remaining attracted to that person. A man would have to spark my intellect and Morris did that for me. We started to say things that established couples would say during a conversation. We bypassed all the game playing, nervousness, and impersonations.

Very rapid and fast moving, our connection became real and relevant in my life. Eventually, we both grew anxious and desired to meet him again (in-person, not online) finally. However, Morris was guarded and questioned the possibility of us. Eight weeks had passed, and it was apparent that we had strong feelings for one another. I was ready to move to another level beyond phone conversations and text messages. Morris' work schedule allowed him the flexibility to function at his own pace. My work week had long, unpredictable hours. However, I knew my schedule in advance and my days off were consistent.

Coming from a small family, Morris liked to keep his private life separate. He was a simple man, yet very charismatic and a deep thinker. I loved that about him! It was natural for me to converse with him. I started to feel the distance becoming farther apart every time I prompted or arranged a place and time for us to meet. We lived in two different cities, but a short plane ride was never out of the question.

The most complicated part of a relationship is expectations. Expectations give you a certain sense of fulfillment and what you want to develop with a certain person. When expectations and needs are not met, there will be heartache and heartbreak. Consistency, loyalty, and love prove the outcome of relationships. I was raised to know that a man is a hunter by nature and when and if he is ready, he would rise to the occasion.

Four months had passed since our initial conversation,

and I felt I had fallen in love with a voice and a few pictures. I was beyond ready to piece my love puzzle together and meet up with my old, but a new found a friend. The first meeting we had planned, Morris never followed through. No phone calls or text messages were returned the day of his anticipated arrival. I began to doubt everything we had built and questioned if it was a lie or a cover-up for something else. What did Morris have going on in his personal life?

Emotionally, I was backed up into a corner. I felt even more distance when I was ignored after our initial meet-up fell apart. At that point, I took my head out of the clouds and opened myself up to the possibilities that Morris was lying. Was this deception? The next day, he finally followed up with a phone call. Morris explained that he wanted to take things slow and continue developing a friendship and foundation before moving forward with anything else. I was perfectly okay with that, but not the disrespect that he showed by avoiding me.

The next week, I answered less of his text messages and phone calls in my usual timely matter. I wanted him to know and feel that if I was not a priority to him then neither should he be to me. This made practical sense. Why should I continue to make someone a priority who only makes me an option? After a week of distance, Morris called and confronted me asking if I was ok because he felt like I was "distant."

Extremely confused, I told him that my time would no longer be devoted to him if he doesn't respect my time. He quickly shot back, "I had to distance myself from us because I'm becoming too attached to you and I don't want to get hurt."

I responded,

"Love is a risk, and you can get hurt in any situation."

Frustrated and on the brink of tears, I told Morris good-bye for the night. Everything seemed like nothing I wanted would come to be. I felt my time, and emotional energy had been wasted.

After another week of digesting the reality that Morris could be untruthful, I became sad again and cut him off completely. Why should I waste my time and energy with someone who clearly isn't ready to build anything and is still playing games? I had invested five months into getting to know him better. I was drained struggling not to answer his phone calls or text messages. I knew time would heal as it had recovered in the past from failed expectations. I tried, but I was getting tired of trying.

Spring swiftly came, and the trees were blooming beautifully. I worked out more on my fitness to keep my mind focused on my goals. I refused to compromise my feelings anymore for someone else's benefit. My summer vacation was right around the corner, and I started making plans. It had been six weeks since I had spoken to Morris. The first week was the longest, but the second week was easier. Although I kept having to remind myself that I was doing this for my benefit in the long run.

On a cloudy Friday in the last week of May, I received an interesting voicemail. Morris had been calling every other day, but I limited my availability. This time I saw he left three voicemails. What could he have to say now?

The first message struck me hard to the core when I pushed play. I heard his voice, but never like this before. It was shaky and unstable. Morris sounded as if he had been crying for hours! The message prompted the word's, "Shanté, I'm sorry for all the pain I've caused you, and it's a direct representation of the pain I have built up over the years. I needed to heal, and I'm sorry for disrespecting you and your time. I love you, and I need to see you as soon as possible."

I connected with his message because it was heartfelt. I knew that he was speaking his truth. Morris had been contemplating on a few things while we weren't talking. I called him back and agreed to meet with him that following Friday. Friday came, yet I didn't get my hopes up. I waited for the phone call from Morris to tell me he was at the airport.

Suddenly, I heard a car door shut outside, and oddly enough another car door shut right after that. I waited by the door and tried to listen to any footsteps or activity. With no windows in sight, it became harder to decipher what exactly was going on outside. I heard a bicycle coming closer and what sounded like six-inch stiletto heels clicking on the pavement.

My phone rang; the voice on the receiver said, "I'm at the door."

I opened the door to find a familiar handsome face man in a suit and tie positioned on one knee with a beautiful Tiffany blue ring box in hand. I was speechless.

Did Morris just catch a flight to see me and now he is proposing marriage? What was I going to do with this? Everything was happening so fast! I flashed a joyful and calm smile and opened my arms for a hug.

Then I had a painful memory resurface. Morris had a temper. Nobody is perfect. There were moments when we would disagree, and I could instantly feel the sting of his rage. Morris would say insensitive things and get very angry. I wasn't sure what would become of his temper. It happened often and questioned if I could make a lifelong commitment to someone so hasty.

I was caught off guard so told Morris to come inside the house. I guess that was not what he wanted to hear. As we sat on the couch, I could see the disappointment in his face. I explained to him that I wanted to grow, take our time, and seek Godly counseling that would guide us in the right direction.

While I didn't say no, it meant not right now. Morris wasn't okay with this. He stormed out of my house and slammed the door. Another episode of Morris' rage. The person that I got to know long distance really started to reveal his true character. The representative that Morris had been putting on the phone was gone.

Morris and I never got married! We tried to continue dating for another month or so. Unfortunately, his character and the amount of growth that he had to do revealed itself. I knew that I could not change him. Morris needed to make the final decision to change and grow for himself.

My gut told me it wasn't a good fit when the first episode of rage showed up. However, I kept on believing that he would change. If a person shows you who they are the first time, believe them! I knew better than to put myself in a position where I was so eager to have a ring just to say that I'm married. I value marriage, but I don't idolize it. So often the woman can find themselves in a toxic marriage because they ignored critical warning signs early on. Some woman may use marriage as a measure to feel validated as a woman. The warning signs were there, and I took note. This relationship could have possibly ended up like my dear friend, Lydia. I know that I made the best choice for me. The lesson in this storm is to have the patience, wisdom, and discernment to make the right choices on who you enter into a relationship with. I desire to have a godly marriage in which we are equally yoked. Don't settle for less because you deserve God's best.

To save yourself from a broken heart, you need to know and understand what's on the other person's heart as soon as possible. Giving your heart to God first is the best way to go. Most importantly, know how to guard your heart. Every compliment you receive doesn't deserve your devotion. God loves you and knows you better than you know yourself. He ensures you that you will never find fault in trusting Him. Your heart will always be safely stowed away in His hands.

There is absolutely nothing wrong with being single and happy at the same time. To be alone and happy is allowing God to prepare you and perfect you as a complete individual. God speaks to you during your alone time. If you can't learn to love spending time with yourself, how can you expect anyone else to?

Self-love is one of the most fulfilling love that you can ever have. I fell in love with myself at an early age. I had a revelation of all that I could contribute to the world and became comfortable with my flaws and my uniqueness. I stood in my individuality. My parents did a great job of validating me before the world could cast any doubt and fears upon me. I knew my worth was priceless, and there was only one of me that existed on this planet. I could never be duplicated, and I would not allow anyone to compare me to someone else.

You have to love your imperfections. I didn't start to genuinely smile until age sixteen. Before then, I was caught up in the flaws of my smile and how the world would receive me. Then I remembered no one else has a smile like mine, and my imperfections are uniquely my own. It's who I am, my identity. Surprisingly, I gained more compliments on my smile once I decided to start smiling! Loving your imperfections and your flaws is what makes you grow and appreciate life.

Healing, Honesty & Honoring Your Wholeness

Healing is a part of life where you must have the power to process the pain and get to the other side. It's finding the beauty that exists in that situation. You should be honest with yourself and what you need in a relationship. Do not settle for less! It's a disservice to settle for less than what you know you deserve. You can't date on potential and hope that someone would one day meet your standards. The desire to have God's best for your life. You will meet people who will amaze you. However, time is the best revelation of true character. Consistency will tell you if it's right for you.

Learn to be okay with being alone. Alone doesn't mean lonely. Utilize your alone time as a time of gratitude. If you are single, you can be happily single. If you are always continually dating or talking to someone, it can serve as a distraction to the work that God is doing in your life. Sometimes God needs to isolate you before He can elevate you. It's those quiet times at night or early in the morning when you can hear God's voice speak to you. He just needs you to be still. Don't drown him out with noise and people who don't honor you or serve a higher purpose in your life.

Keep friends who honor, love and value you. You may have "friends" who tolerate you because of what you can do for them. They want your companionship, to hang out with them or make them smile and laugh. Friends shouldn't use you or be fair weathered. They should be there during the good and bad times. A friend that can't weather the storms of your life is not a friend, that's an associate. Who's really riding it out with you?

Often, it's what you don't do that makes you who you are. It's inevitable that you will face difficult decisions that could impact your entire life with a simple "yes" or "no" answer. Don't feel pressured to conform to the ways of others. If what people are telling you don't align with your values, character or your purpose, then don't do it! Be ok with being a unique person who paves your own way. Real friends will not make you feel bad or pressure you when you desire to stay in your lane and make the best choices for yourself. Be open to allowing yourself time to heal. It requires work to be open to going through the hurt, pain, and the pressure of a setback from the storm. Just ride it out!

You cannot fix what you do not confront head-on. Seek counseling to talk about your pain, or it will continually reappear throughout your life. Once you complete this process, it helps you to become a healthy person that you need to be.

You cannot be completely present in a relationship or serve any good to others if you are not good to yourself. Beauty shines from within, and your ability to love and accept yourself with all the flaws helps to fulfill your own potential. This constitutes wholeness.

Many people drown their pain in drugs, sex, alcohol or displaced anger and rage. Don't mistake a temporary high for an escape. These vices are destructive. They fail to promote growth and restoration. They only mask some underlying problems. Live above the influence of harming yourself and be courageous enough to expose the real issue that lies beneath the surface.

Houston Strong

"There is more love in Houston than water"
~ Unknown

As I parked my car, a lady in another car across the street waved at me excitedly from the church parking lot. I had no idea who she was. As she strolled towards me, her smiling face became recognizable. It was one of my good friends, Maria. I gave Maria a huge hug, and we caught up about life. She didn't stop smiling. Minutes later, I found out that her house was underwater from Hurricane Harvey. Maria and her husband had lost nearly EVERYTHING! They just purchased their first home a few months prior. My heart sank into my chest. I knew what it felt like lose almost everything. I had been there before with Hurricane Katrina. I gave her another hug and stared into her eyes. I could tell she was still in shock.

When devastation strikes, you go into a pause and panic phase. Maria was suffering an incredible loss. I completely understood. I had lost so much in Hurricane Katrina, but my life was saved. I knew that God had timed Maria and me to connect at that exact time and location.

I had just returned home from Dallas. Only days ago, I had evacuated Houston at a moment's notice to escape the impending destruction of Hurricane Harvey. Before the emergency sirens even sounded, I was proactive and evacuated the city without hesitation. I was well-prepared to ride out another big storm. A category 4 to be exact! When a catastrophic storm reoccurs in your life, you still have to ride it out. It took about a week before it was safe enough for me to come back home to Houston. When the coast was clear, I went straight to church for a much needed a dose of hope.

Two years earlier, on the very day Hurricane Harvey hit down in Houston, I made the city my home. The town had the progress, southern hospitality, cultural diversity, growth, and speed that I was looking for. I knew Houston was something special. I felt it there upon my first visit. I was looking for a place to call home one last time. I had relocated enough moving from city to city because of school, work, and career opportunities. I was so grateful for these experiences, but it was time for me to find a permanent place that matched my long-term interests. Houston had the vibe I loved and offered opportunities for me to achieve even higher goals.

As a new Houstonian, I was finally home, and this was my final stop. Once again, I found myself residing on the gulf coast. The possibility of experiencing another hurricane definitely crossed my mind. However, I felt any geographic location had its challenges with natural disasters from earthquakes to hurricanes or from tornadoes to monsoons. After all, what are the chances that I would suffer and survive two high category hurricanes in my lifetime?

Maria and I continued to make our way into the church service to give thanks and praise to God. It was an emotionally charged service. The sermon was on hope, love, and honoring those who sacrificed their lives and time to help rescue the city of Houston. It was a miracle that I was sitting in a church that was surrounded by water several days before. It only took the church seven days after the storm to open its door in serving its members and neighbors.

The outpour of support and heroic efforts were beyond phenomenal! I was shocked at the timeliness of the city's response to getting back on its feet. Hurricane Harvey brought over 50 inches of water to Houston. It displaced more than 1 million people and damaged some 200,000 homes in a path of destruction stretching for more than 300 miles. Hurricane Harvey went down as one of the most dangerous storms in U.S. history causing an estimated $180 billion in damages and the lives of at least 50 people and counting.[v]

A natural disaster knows no race or color. When such tragedy strikes, your life is threatened regardless of what you look like. This is the time for humanity and the hero within to arise. What amazed me the most was the response level of humanity and activism I saw amongst strangers. Houston came out to help Houston! Neighboring states also came out to support the city and other gulf coast areas in need. True compassion of humanity was on display. This showed me that

Houston's darkest hour was also its finest hour. It made me proud to say, I live here. Help didn't have a race, religion or political belief. If you needed help in Houston, you were going to receive it! I saw boats lined up on the freeway to rescue those who were flooded from Hurricane Harvey. This caused me to connect with Houston even deeper. Again, I was home.

When I first heard of Hurricane Harvey, I instantly felt ripples of chills and had flashbacks from Hurricane Katrina. While I knew how to ride it out, this time I was wiser. I knew that I didn't have to weather the storm, in the same manner, I did over a decade ago. Hurricane Katrina gave me the wisdom to bypass Hurricane Harvey in a better way. Before any announcements were made of emergency evacuations, I evacuated myself and my mom. She had recently moved to Houston to be closer to me.

I felt no panic or anxiety about being disconnected from my materials at home. The safety of my mom and myself was a top priority over everything. There will always be items that we cannot replace. Everything cannot be saved in the iCloud. Although I had to gain strength once again to let go and trust God. He always provides for you!

I felt so much stronger this time around. Storms shift your perspective and challenge your faith. You may be in a situation right now in which your house, car or material possessions are destroyed. It's important to know that the home that God wants to build for you is far greater than anything Home Depot can supply.

Change is unavoidable, but growth is possible. I've shared the real-life storms that I've survived to be an encouragement to you. My hope is for you to understand that life is full of swift transitions and challenges. They are many different kinds of storms such as financial, physical, emotional, invisible or internal. Storms will try to drown you to death, but you can survive when you realize that very storm serves a purpose.

When I was able to get my head above water eventually, I soon discovered purpose in the Category 5 hurricanes, sudden traffic stops, unjustified arrests, challenging competitions, crazy car accidents, adapting to transitions or going through toxic relationships. What I learned is that YOU HAVE TO RIDE IT OUT!

Although you may not realize why you go through the hardships that you do, I'm a firm believer that God has handpicked these events for you to build the character, tenacity, and strength you need to succeed in life. If I had not gone through these storms, I would not be the same person I am today. The way I handle stress and adversity now is entirely different from how I managed it ten years ago. My temperament is a direct reflection of that.

When you think of the hardships that have caused turmoil or trauma in your life, you should value the gifts that you've been given when you make it through. Believe and know that you can get through any storm as long as you ride it out. You have the innate ability to rise above your circumstances, if and only if you first change your mindset. Having a positive mental attitude is necessary for success.

I attracted and attained success once I developed a positive mental attitude. I also created a routine of self- care that enabled me to get to a place of peace and harmony in the world and connect with my inner core. The daily demands of work, family, and life, in general, can take a toll on you. However, you are in control of your own emotions, body, and well-being. You can decide what relationships you involve yourself in, what foods you eat, what degree you seek, which job to take and where your future will go. Greatness is your choice, and you decide the way forward.

The words in this memoir are the hardest words I've ever written because I had to revisit and reflect on some of the most painful periods in my life. These painful memories have helped me unfold the pages of this book to tell the story of the most progressive periods in my life. What's the narrative of your own story? Can you see the beauty in your pain? Pain can serve as God's form of protection. I think of it as a warning or a call-to-action to do something differently.

If you find yourself in multiple storms throughout your life, remember my words, ride it out! You can channel the storms into greatness far beyond your expectations. Nobody can stop you from dreaming and reaching your goals, but you. If you believe that you are capable or not, you are correct. Make your mind up today that you can do all things, remember, there is no storm that you cannot face.

Knowing who you are is reassuring in the tests, trials, and setbacks that are a definitive part of life. God has equipped you with everything you need to survive. He enables you to bear up under your burdens by His grace. Never forget that God has handpicked your circumstances to accomplish a specific purpose. Your life has no finish line.

The progress, blessings, and miracles are on the other side of your doubt, fear, stagnancy, and the ability to ride it out. I am a living testimony that you can turn your pain into progress, your misery into miracles, and your setbacks into setups to come back stronger and better.

Today you have witnessed snapshots of my journey. I want you to know that storms don't happen for you, but it happens to you. Your life starts now! Not next year, next summer, when you get married, when you get more money, a new job, or a new degree. Those things certainly add definition and meaning to your life, but you have to put the most value in knowing that there is nobody like you on earth. No one can write your story and live your life, but you! You are fully capable of transforming your storms into greatness and mastering your purpose. Life is always going to have storms, but the beauty is always in you riding it out.

Acknowledgements

Thank you God for blessing me to see this journey complete. May this book go on to inspire greatness, impact lives, and empower youth, young adults, and anybody that may face a storm in their life. I understand I am the vessel and messenger of the great works that you are doing within me.

Mother, thank you for your love, care, concern and your endless phone calls throughout Hurricane Katrina. Who knew that phone call would spark the title of my first book!? Thank you for your godly counsel, wisdom and always praying for me. Daddy, thank you for your protection, care, love, and millions of lectures via car, plane, train or bus! You never stopped believing in me and helped me find power in my own voice. Continue to push Jhaylen and Jhordan towards greatness like you did me! I thank both of my parents for nurturing me and helping me grow into the responsible adult that I am today.

My awesome brothers, Tony, Jhaylen, and Jhordan. I love you. Thanks for riding it out always and forever. Jhaylen and Jhordan you are the future. I expect nothing but greatness from you. Stay positive and progressive and listen to your Daddy! :)

Uncle Kevin, "Unc" and family thank you for pushing me towards greatness. Thank you for your warm hospitality throughout my duration in L.A. I've always been inspired by you and your insightful words, radical preaching, and realistic perspectives over a variety issues. Keep preaching and keep writing!

Ms. Edna Martin, thank you for being an awesome high school guidance counselor. Thank you for helping me write my first powerful college essay and for tolerating me bugging you in high school. I was focused and I needed scholarships! You help me see myself at another level. Thank for your guidance, positivity, and direction.

Dr. Gwendolyn Packnett, thank you for your care and concern as a counselor post-Katrina. You made my transition to UMSL and back home a comfortable one. The time you spent with made a world of a difference in my growth and healing during my transition.

Mrs. Kim Anderson "Mama Kim", thank you for putting the pressure on me every time we spoke and yelling at me, "Where is my book?!" I love that you never lost sight of my goals even when I became discouraged or distracted at times. I'm immensely inspired by you. Thank you for being an awesome mentor, friend and coach.

Mrs. Cherie Banks, thank you for being an awesome mentor and friend. Thank you for building a platform in Phoenix that allowed me to share my words through expressing my poetry. Where would I have met you I wonder?! Your words that you poured into me spoke volumes and help me get past some major roadblocks with Ride It Out. Thank you.

Thank you to all of my dedicated professors and teachers at my prior learning institutions: Gateway Middle School, Gateway Institute of Technology High School, Xavier University of Louisiana, Tulane University, and University of Missouri-Saint Louis. Thank you for your wisdom and many lessons taught.

Thank you to the team at Essence Magazine that inspired, educated, and instilled in me professional expertise that every young writer should have. Throughout my impactful internship I gained insight that completely transformed and stretched me.

To team Ride It Out, thank you to my amazing team. You pushed me to go to places that I really didn't want to go and write from a deeper perspective. It wasn't easy but I'm sure it's worth it.

To my beautiful family, friends, sister-friends, colleagues, supporters! I love you all so much for contributing your words of encouragement along this journey. Ride It Out is so important to me, and you have supported the process, understood, and respected my struggles along the way.

With much love and gratitude,
Shanté Denise Lynn Berry

A note about the author

Shanté Berry is a writer, poet, mentor, social entrepreneur, public speaker and a catalyst for positive change. She is a product of the Saint Louis Public Schools system. She graduated from Gateway Institute of Technology High School and Xavier University of Louisiana. She has worked and written for Essence Magazine and developed her own editorial blogs. She is also a finance specialist working in the field of education. Driven by her obstacles and miracles in life, she transforms everything she has experienced into motivation for herself and others to succeed. She has a deep passion for health, literacy & continuing a legacy of excellence. She seeks to empower and enhance her community through literacy, mentoring, and motivation. She loves spending time with her family, laughing, writing, and traveling. She believes that literacy can change lives and if you open a book, your world will open as well. Ms. Berry currently resides in Texas.

Endnotes

i.   Jolley, Willie (2000) A setback is a setup for a comeback. New York, NY: St. Martin's Griffin

ii.   Bradbury, Ray. "A sound of thunder." Colliers Magazine, June 1952

iii.   http://www.nytimes.com/1992/05/03/us/riot-los-angles-overview-cleanup-begins-los-angeles-enforce-surreal-calm.html?pagewanted=all

iv.   Starks, Glen. (2017) *African American by the Numbers* Santa Barbara, CA:ABC-CLIO

v.   Starks, Glen. (2017) *African American by the Numbers* Santa Barbara, CA:ABC-CLIO

vi.   Advanced feature in ancestry composition" 23andMe https://you.23andme.com/reports/ancestry_composition/Accessed 17 September 2013

vii.   Les Brown – "You have the power to change." Les Brown Enterprises. Accessed18 August 2014

viii. New Intentional Version Bible, 1978 (Proverbs 23:7)

ix.   The Bishop of Geneva, Saint Francis de Sales (1567-1622)

x.   http://fortune.com/2017/09/03/hurricane-harvey-damages-cost/Accessed September, 2017

Made in the USA
Columbia, SC
05 November 2021

48422726R00098